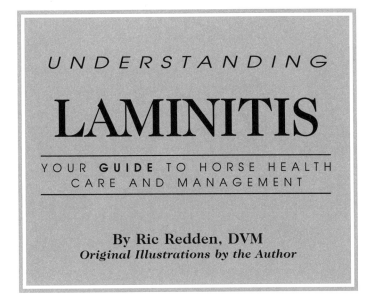

UNDERSTANDING

LAMINITIS

YOUR **GUIDE** TO HORSE HEALTH
CARE AND MANAGEMENT

By Ric Redden, DVM
Original Illustrations by the Author

The Blood-Horse, Inc. Lexington, KY

Other titles offered by
The Horse Health Care Library

Understanding EPM

Understanding Equine Lameness

Understanding Equine First Aid

Understanding The Equine Foot

Understanding Equine Nutrition

UNDERSTANDING

LAMINITIS

YOUR **GUIDE** TO HORSE HEALTH
CARE AND MANAGEMENT

ISBN 0-939049-98-8

Printed in the United States of America

First Edition: August 1998

1 2 3 4 5 6 7 8 9 10

Contents

INTRODUCTION

Every day I get calls from veterinarians, owners and farriers from all over the world. They all have questions about laminitis. Many of these people are concerned because their horses are not responding to traditional treatments. They say they need help desperately. Owners ask, "What can I do for my horse?"

Everyone should be concerned about laminitis because it is a devastating disease that strikes all breeds of horses regardless of their age or use. It can afflict a multi-million-dollar racehorse, a show jumper, or a child's pony. Laminitis can be triggered by any number of things: overeating and obesity, another disease such as colic, a troubled foaling, or a leg injury.

Whatever the cause, it always involves the foot. It always involves emotion because of the relationship between the owner and horse, whether the horse is worth six figures or has little monetary value. The onset of laminitis is always an equine emergency. It should be treated as an emergency because it can quickly annihilate the career, or in many cases take the life of, the horse in a matter of days or weeks. But it doesn't have to be this way.

Unfortunately, misconceptions abound about laminitis, which often is referred to in lay terms as founder. Most horse owners do not have a basic understanding of the equine foot. One misconception is that if you take away all the horse's feed and only feed it grass hay and water, the horse will eventually get well. Here's another misconception: if you walk a laminitic horse continuously, around the clock, or tie it out in the creek for three days, then it will recuperate. Wrong!

Treating laminitis successfully requires a basic understanding of the anatomy, physiology, and functions of the equine foot, plus a mechanical understanding of how the sensitive structures in the foot relate to the movement of the horse.

In *Understanding Laminitis*, you will learn how to spot the signs of laminitis. You will get an anatomy lesson in order to learn what happens inside the foot when laminitis strikes. You also will learn that sometimes you can reverse the damaging forces and treat laminitis successfully. I will describe specific cases and constantly reinforce the basic mechanical principles that I use with consistent success to save the careers, as well as the lives, of very important horses.

I had my first exposure to laminitis in 1964, when I bought my first horse. I was a very young farrier. I enjoyed riding and living in a 24-hour-a-day horse world. Then, my first horse developed laminitis. As in many other cases of laminitis, my horse was fine one day and dead lame the next. Being exposed to other horses with acute laminitis gave me fresh insights about what was happening to my mare's feet and what was ahead. Her hard days were yet to come.

Until that time, I had never really thought about what I would do to pull a horse through a laminitic episode. I called in two local veterinarians to treat my mare. They treated all types of animals but did not have much experience with horses, much less horses with acute laminitis. Both of them suggested things that might work. Ultimately, I was still left without a specific, detailed means of treating her. So I watched her. At first, her feet were so painful that she couldn't stand up. For the first few days, she was very reluctant to pick up her feet. When I felt them they were red hot.

"Just tie her in the creek. It might help," I was told, so I did and standing her in the pond for 48 hours did give her some relief. That experiment made me aware that she wanted her heels elevated because when she stood in the mud, she was immediately more comfortable. The impression that she made in the mud showed her toes were pointed almost straight down.

Thinking mechanically, I wondered if I could position her foot with her heel elevated just as it had been while she stood in the mud. I thought maybe she would like that. So I did, making wooden wedges and nailing them to her feet. The higher I made them, the better she liked it. She responded favorably over the next 72 hours. Her condition continued to improve. Within three months I was riding her as if nothing had ever happened to her.

This very interesting, hit-home case made me aware of how devastating the laminitis syndrome can be and how little we know about it. I started looking for laminitic horses to shoe because it gave me a very good feeling of accomplishment when the mechanical remedies I used worked so well, although I didn't fully understand why. At about the same time, a theory was introduced by a researcher at the University of Pennsylvania New Bolton Center. His concept was to lower the heels drastically as an aid in treating acute laminitis. Over the next few years, as a farrier working with several Kentucky veterinarians on extremely valuable animals, I used this technique with some degree of success.

In the early 1970s, when I entered the College of Veterinary Medicine at The Ohio State University, this special shoeing technique was still considered to be the best choice of treatment for laminitic horses. I worked very hard trying to believe in it, but I found that lowering the heels only succeeded with a small percentage of the cases that were treated at The Ohio State veterinary hospital. The vast majority of laminitic cases resulted in frustration for the clients and sometimes devastating consequences for the horses.

When I was in vet school, it occurred to me that I needed to go back and examine the experience I had with my own mare. I applied the medical knowledge that I had learned while in professional school to the simple mechanics I used to reverse the forces at play that were crippling my mare. When I graduated in 1974 with an award of distinction for excellence in equine surgery and medicine, I felt that I was ready to tackle the world. Little did I know that my learning days had just begun.

Developing effective treatment protocols for laminitis became my goal. It has become my life's work. I have dedicated the last 25 years to treating this devastating disease and developing a precise mechanical protocol to help others. I have worked on laminitis cases with veterinarians, farriers, owners, and insurance companies in 19 countries and across America and I continue to teach my methods at several symposiums and workshops. I also describe my techniques in magazine articles. One of the main points I make in every speech and article is that we do not need to reinvent the wheel with every single case of laminitis, but simply follow basic principles of physics.

After treating hundreds and hundreds of laminitic horses, I know that certain treatment regimens work when designed to a specific purpose and that they work again and again. I have also learned that this is a very complex syndrome and that we have much to learn and that there are cases that are totally non-responsive, despite our efforts. This book is a guide that will lead you through the basic thinking process that has evolved into my current, very straight-forward yet simple, protocol for treating this devastating disease. I will help you bypass the many, many wrong turns that I have made in spite of my sincerity in seeking the right answers.

Ric Redden, DVM
Versailles, Kentucky

CHAPTER 1

What Is Laminitis?

The word laminitis elicits fear among horsemen because many associate it with the end of a horse's career and sometimes the horse's life. Laminitis is a catastrophic event that should always be treated as an emergency. Recent research and new techniques used to treat this condition now make it possible to save horses that might have died or been euthanized. A diagnosis of laminitis no longer has to be a death sentence.

What is laminitis? Simply put, laminitis is an inflammation of the laminae, the sensitive tissues that connect the hoof wall to the coffin bone and other structures of the horse's foot. The laminae play a major role in stabilizing the bones inside the foot. When inflammation occurs, the integrity of this crucial bond is often compromised, leading to very serious damage to the bones and soft tissues.

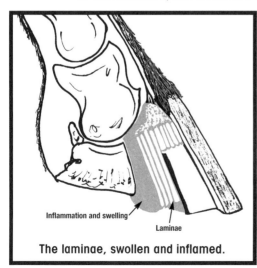

Inflammation and swelling
Laminae

The laminae, swollen and inflamed.

Laminitis can strike any horse regardless of its breed,

use, or activity. It mostly occurs in mature horses and is rarely found in horses less than a year old. In my many years of practice, I have never seen a case where the laminitis is the primary disease. It has always been secondary to another disease process or trauma. Sometimes, the feet of a horse become involved as result of another disease process, such as colic, Potomac horse fever, or salmonella.

Recent research has provided greater insights to explain what is actually happening to the blood supply within the foot and how that affects the integrity of the structure.

> ## AT A GLANCE
>
> - Laminitis is inflammation of the laminae, sensitive tissues that connect the hoof wall to the coffin bone and other structures in the foot.
>
> - The blood supply in the foot is reduced or compromised in the laminitic foot, leading to cell death.
>
> - Laminitis can strike any breed of horse, but mostly occurs in mature horses.

It's important to have a better understanding of the mechanics of the foot and the forces at play concerning the normal foot as well as the laminitic foot. This understanding gives the treatment team consisting of a veterinarian, a farrier, and the horse's owner the means to reverse those forces that can damage the foot during a laminitis episode. Inflammation of the laminae leads to ischemia, which is simply cell death. The cells die because they cannot obtain nutrients from the blood supply. The blood is shunted away from the foot by a mechanism that is not fully understood. However, we do know that the reduced blood supply sets the stage for in-

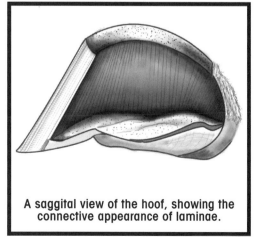

A saggital view of the hoof, showing the connective appearance of laminae.

flammation and subsequent cell death, which destroys the intricate network of laminae as this tissue suspends the horse's weight between the coffin bone and the hoof wall.

Laminae act like the tiny hooks and grippers in Velcro strips when they have been fastened together. One side is attached to the bone, the other side to the wall. If all of the laminae were placed flat, their surface area would approximately equal the size of a tennis court. For this reason, a horse can suffer from laminitis and have a very mild insult to a very small area of the total surface. Another laminitic horse might have a very severe insult that wipes out the majority of this laminae within hours, leading to a catastrophic situation as the hoof wall separates from the foot.

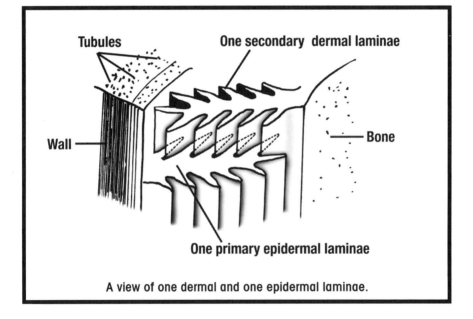

A view of one dermal and one epidermal laminae.

BASIC STEPS OF PROGRESSIVE DISEASE

Laminitis can be triggered by a variety of factors. A conscientious owner or manager should be alert to the following because the history that you give to your veterinarian could have key implications for the diagnosis as well as the prognosis. Common primary problems that often precede laminitis are:

- Over eating grain or grass (especially by obese animals).
- Prolonged high fever.
- Severe colic.
- Retained placenta; 12 hours-plus can precipitate the onset of laminitis.
- Pneumonia.
- Pleuritis.
- Potomac horse fever.
- Salmonella colitis.
- Stress, brought on by constant movement, shipping, show stress, loss of sleep, water deprivation, or dehydration.
- Unilateral lameness. When a horse suffers a severe injury in one leg or foot, it can develop laminitis in the opposing limb by trying to keep weight off the injured limb.

Whatever the cause and degree of severity, laminitis is always an emergency. We'll look at some of the signs and typical scenarios in the next chapter.

CHAPTER 2

What Are The Signs Of Laminitis?

The most common sign of the onset of laminitis is lameness. If the horse can be persuaded to walk, it moves with a shortened stride, with each foot quickly placed back on the ground. Standing still, the horse appears to have its "feet nailed to the floor" in the parlance of old-time horsemen. The characteristic stance of a laminitic horse includes hind feet brought forward under its belly to get most of its weight off its front feet, which are stuck out in front of its normal center of gravity. If all four feet are affected and the horse is in severe pain, it might lie down and be reluctant to get up again.

This horse is displaying the characteristic stance of laminitis.

On closer examination, you may find that the horse has a bounding pulse. Always check the pulse before moving the animal, because even in a healthy horse, a few steps can increase the pressure within the blood vessels.

There are cases of severe, acute laminitis in which the pulse is very faint or not detectable at all. Most have warmer than normal feet. But in rare cases, they can be ice cold as well. Therefore, you must use other clinical signs if you have a suspected case of laminitis. The most obvious sign is acute lameness or signs of pain. You most likely have an emergency. Even if the horse ultimately does not have laminitis, its pain requires prompt attention, so call your veterinarian and your farrier. Ask them to come out to see the horse right away. You want to include your farrier because he or she knows your horse's feet better than you do and can be extremely helpful in telling the veterinarian what changes might be noticeable.

> ## AT A GLANCE
>
> • A horse suffering from laminitis often is reluctant to move.
>
> • The laminitic horse often has a characteristic stance.
>
> • The digital pulse can be bounding.
>
> • One or more feet can be affected.
>
> • Be alert to any changes which could have precipitated the onset of laminitis.

The quicker you get help for your horse, the greater the chances that the horse will recover. Help means treating the acute inflammatory stage as well as the inciting cause, and mechanically reversing the forces at play that are working to destroy the vital, sensitive areas inside the foot. It's vitally important for your vet and farrier to work together at this point to treat this potentially devastating disease.

Therapy that's initiated the moment the horse shows the slightest sign of laminitis increases the window of response time so critical to the horse's recovery.

ESTABLISH THE GRADE OF LAMENESS

It helps to be able to tell your vet how lame your horse is. There are several published grading systems referring to lameness in general. However, it's helpful to differentiate the degree of lameness in the context of possible laminitis.

Grade 1) Walks sound, trots lame, turns sore. You can readily pick up any of the four feet.

Grade 2) Walks sore, turns on hind feet, reluctant to trot. Reluctant to have feet picked up.

Grade 3) Refusing to trot. Has to be persuaded to walk. Very reluctant to have feet picked up.

Grade 4) Stands with feet rooted to the ground. Reluctant to move even with strong persuasion. Refuses to have feet picked up. Very painful facial expression. If lying down, very difficult to make them get up.

Industry wide statistics are not very encouraging as far as prognosis is concerned and many veterinarians worldwide consider complicated laminitis akin to a death sentence. A majority of laminitic cases recover using various means of treatment — some even without treatment — and seem to suffer no ill consequences. However, 20% to 30% of the across-the-board cases will have a very devastating insult, resulting in catastrophic damage to the laminae, costing either careers or lives.

Try to establish the grade of lameness.

A lackadaisical approach to this syndrome works well if you have a very mild insult. But unfortunately it is impossible to differentiate between mild and complicated cases at the onset of the syndrome. If you treat the complicated case as you would a mild case, you essentially have destroyed your chances of saving the career or even the life of the horse.

In my experience, I have had good success rates with complicated cases using a disciplined, methodical approach. I will describe those methods later in this book.

LAMINITIS CAN STRIKE ONE OR ALL FEET

Many people think laminitis is caused only by overeating and that it always involves the two front feet. Therefore, it is unlikely for them to suspect that a multitude of other problems can cause laminitis. While overeating grain or grass can cause laminitis, commonly resulting in lameness in the front two feet, there are numerous other causes that are just as prevalent and every conceivable combination of feet — from one to four — can be involved. Cases involving a single foot, called unilateral laminitis, are quite common. Laminitis involving both hind feet with no front feet involvement is rare. When it occurs, damage can range from mild to severe.

The degree of damage varies considerably from case to case and is influenced by the severity of the insult at the onset. Due to the complexity of the syndrome and response to therapy, I have found it impossible to describe a single set of signs, or a preferred treatment protocol yielding a good response.

Therefore, to help you understand laminitis, I will make references to specific signs that are representative of the basic categories of this syndrome. Each example will be described as to its characteristics, signs, symptoms, history, response to treatment, and prognosis for recovery.

To talk specifically about laminitis, you will need a point of reference. Trying to lump all of the possible variables and all cases into the single, broad category of laminitis becomes very confusing to owners, veterinarians, and farriers and leaves us without a meaningful way to initiate a precise treatment regime for a specific case. After 25 years of extensive experience, I have found this blanket approach to be the main reason the prognosis for complicated cases has always been so poor.

To make your in-depth study of laminitis more productive, consider the following "typical" laminitis scenarios.

EXAMPLE # 1 (TYPICAL ACUTE)

In this example, we start with a fit and healthy horse which has been in rigorous training, either for racing or some other type of athletic competition. The horse is handled and observed on a daily basis, so that the changes would be noticed almost immediately.

It began showing a marked reluctance to move in the stall or to walk out of the stall. When the horse was encouraged to move forward, its head went up, its hind legs traveled under the abdomen, and its front legs moved forward in a very stiff fashion.

The horse's eyes told a painful story. Its respiration and heart rate increased. The horse seemed "nailed to the floor," exhibiting signs of distress when you tried to pick up either front foot (one is usually more painful). The feet seemed warmer than normal, but since the feet of some laminitis cases remain quite cool to the touch, this was not a reliable sign.

When you checked the digital pulse it seemed quite strong.

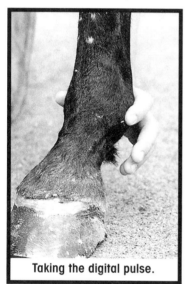

Taking the digital pulse.

To feel for the pulse, reach down and lightly touch the vessels where they course over the back corner of the fetlock. There the digital vein, artery, and nerve can be found under the skin. It is the artery that has the bounding pulse, if it exists.

In a healthy horse, the normal resting pulse can be very difficult to detect and you must have a very light touch in order to feel it. Regularly checking the pulse of your horse helps you better understand the range of normal. In a laminitic horse, the pressure with every pulse beat seems to thump hard against your thumb and forefinger. The heart rate might be normal or elevated, but it's the increased pressure within the vessel that we're actually feeling.

It is thought by some horsemen as well as some professionals that a mild case of laminitis doesn't warrant immediate treatment as they have had good prior experience treating this syndrome with various conservative methods. Unfortunately, in the early stages of the syndrome, there is no way of determining the course of events that lies ahead for your horse. If you decide to risk playing the odds and do not immediately treat the laminitis syndrome aggressively and there has been a very significant insult to the laminae, you have lost a large majority of the window of time where prompt treatment can make the biggest difference.

Treating complicated cases aggressively from the onset does not guarantee you with favorable results as cases with massive lamellar death at the time of onset can be non-responsive to the most aggressive of techniques. On the other hand, using a maximum mechanical and therapeutic treatment regime at the outset offers unlimited options that are not available with a more conservative approach. Treating a horse with great hope of total recovery in this fashion assures you that you're doing everything possible and, barring unforeseen setbacks due to vascular collapse, your end results can be very favorable.

LOOKING FOR CLUES

Early treatment is designed not only to attack the syndrome but to prevent the secondary mechanical destruction. While you wait for your veterinarian and farrier to arrive, review what might have prompted the onset of laminitis. Consider what occurred the previous 48 to 72 hours. Did your horse travel and have a stressful trip? Did it have a high fever or signs of labored breathing? Has it been exposed to conditions that might precipitate pneumonia or some other respiratory disease? Has one or more of its limbs become swollen for apparently no reason? Has the horse recently received an influenza vaccination or any other kind of injection? Has the horse recently been given corticosteroids?

AT A GLANCE

- Has your horse traveled or undergone any stress?

- Contracted or been exposed to a respiratory disease?

- Recently received innoculations or injections?

- Been administered corticosteroid injections?

- Eaten an abnormally large amount of food?

Although treating horses with corticosteroids can have very beneficial effects, I advise caution. A small percentage of horses have developed laminitis within a few hours to a few days following corticosteriod therapy. Many veterinarians believe that there is a direct correlation. Even though the incidence is quite low, I am among many veterinarians who believe there is an inherent risk in such treatments and therefore caution is advised when using corticosteroids.

Note: As far as steroid therapy, we basically have two: (1) corticosteroids (such as Dexamethasone, Depo-Medrol, Vetalog, etc.) have potent anti-inflammatory properties indicated for numerous uses; and (2) anabolic steroids (including Winstrol-V, Equipoise, and others), which are used to increase appetite, stimulate muscle development, and are hormonal in nature. Anabolic steroids should not be confused with corticosteroids.

Has your horse inadvertently consumed a much larger amount of grain than it normally eats? Many horses require tremendous amounts of grain to maintain peak condition, whereas others might need only a handful. When a horse manages to break into the feed room, it might eat only what it needs while others will gorge until they have consumed all of the grain. If a horse devours too much grain, you have a major problem. Call your veterinarian immediately as swift action cannot only prevent gastritis and subsequent laminitis but it might save the life of your animal.

Other things to consider:

When was your horse last shod? Did your farrier have any problems or comments concerning the feet? Your farrier most likely knows the unique characteristics of your horse's feet much better than you, which is invaluable when assessing the degree of damage. Things the farrier might look for: increased sensitivity around the coronary band; changes in the coronary band itself, such as swelling or discharge or moisture that might indicate serum leakage or a possible abscess; an abnormal ledge formation or an abnormally distinct margin to the hoof wall; increased sensitivity over the sole and toe area detected through use of a hoof tester.

Has the conformation of the sole changed? Is the sole sagging, does it seem to be fuller? Is the sole bruised? The farrier might pull the shoe to better inspect the area under the shoe for hot nails and other shoeing-related problems. His or her findings become invaluable in helping the veterinarian interpret the visual as well as radiographic evidence of a potential problem.

The veterinarian will assess the overall health of the animal in an effort to rule out underlying metabolic problems that could possibly have precipitated the acute signs of pain. It is extremely important to address the seat of the problem if it can be diagnosed.

When nothing out of the ordinary has occurred, consider whether your horse has experienced stress. This could be stress from traveling, any change in routine, or changes in feed or water. Veterinarians have long acknowledged a link between stress and the onset of laminitis.

We are aware of certain disease syndromes that can precipitate laminitis, but it's difficult to relate known causes to a particular case. Owners and trainers are distraught thinking they have done something wrong because they can't pinpoint a precise reason for the horse showing laminitic signs. You don't need to know the reason to try to resolve the problem. It can be a helpful indicator to what lies ahead, but close observation of the horse, radiographs, and response to therapy is more valuable than knowing precisely what caused it.

EXAMPLE # 2 (UNILATERAL LAMINITIS)

In this example, the horse has a very serious injury in one leg, which leaves him quite lame for several weeks, regardless of treatment, consequently causing him to bear full weight on the opposing limb throughout the recovery. Treating the original injury in successful fashion is one thing, but protecting the

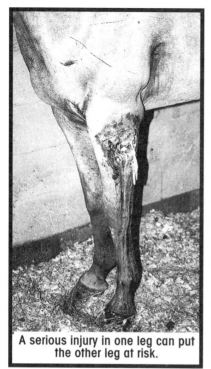

A serious injury in one leg can put the other leg at risk.

other foot from opposing limb laminitis is quite another. Many cases of acute unilateral lameness develop complicated opposing limb laminitis within six to eight weeks of injury. This problem occurs because the horse shifts its weight to that sound limb to relieve pain and pressure on the injured or sore leg. Constant and chronic weight bearing on one limb severely compromises normal blood flow to the laminae and precipitates local ischemic laminitis.

Anticipating potential laminitis in the supporting foot helps us to become alert to subtle changes in stance, shifting back and forth, increased pulse, and other clinical signs. If you wait until the horse is favoring the good limb and putting full support on the injured leg before employing mechanical aids, the prognosis is severely jeopardized.

Other signs of opposing limb laminitis include a ledge along the coronary band, which is a sharp, protruding edge of the wall. The ledge can be confirmed radiographically. The horse's coffin bone has slipped down into the hoof capsule (we call this a sinker). You also might find serum (yellow fluid) oozing from the coronary band. The sole can be flat or bulging down. Palpating the coronary band daily on high-risk patients will help you notice subtle changes which can save your horse's life.

Another typical sign is for the horse to jerk the good foot up, momentarily, as if it were stinging. It then might develop a consistent shifting leg lameness. The foot is in serious jeopardy.

Horses with weak, thin hoof capsules, toe cracks, and other previous injuries or disease are at a much higher risk of traumatic laminitis than those with strong, durable feet. This is important to recognize and efforts should be made to protect the opposing foot mechanically from the ill effects of prolonged, excessive loading. Fortunately, many of these catastrophic injuries can be treated successfully in four to six weeks. Unfortunately, that's about the time the good foot crashes with a devastating case of laminitis.

In my experience, light-boned fillies tend to have a higher incidence of traumatic laminitis than do colts and mature horses. It is not unusual to see it within two weeks following an acute injury. A large percentage of traumatic laminitic cases can be prevented with early mechanical aids

EXAMPLE # 3 (HIND LIMB LAMINITIS)

Hind limb laminitis might not occur as frequently as front limb, but it does happen and it is as much of an emergency. Being alert to the early signs can improve the prognosis.

Horses suffering from hind limb laminitis stand with their hind legs stretched out behind them. They look as if they want to urinate. They will tread back and forth, but are reluctant to move forward. This type of laminitis is difficult to detect early. In fact, it is often misdiagnosed, or mistaken for other problems such as kidney problems or acute back pain. Sometimes the horses will appear to have signs of a neurological disorder such as you may find with EPM (equine protozoal myeloencephalitis). Being aware that hind limb laminitis does exist should become a valuable part of the tentative diagnosis. It should certainly prompt those emergency calls to the veterinarian and farrier. They will thoroughly check the horse's feet with hoof testers and radiographs.

EXAMPLE # 4 (OBESITY)

It's springtime and the grass is long and lush and you are proud that all your horses look great. But there is a likelihood that they are all quite heavy. When they start consuming spring grass that might contain up to 35% protein, they gain several pounds every day. Suddenly, your favorite horse shows acute signs of laminitis. It's standing with its hind feet pulled under its body and is reluctant to move.

Overweight ponies and horses are at high risk of laminitis because fat storage increases the risk of carbohydrate overload, which can trigger the laminitis. Remember that the perception of what's obese and what's not is viewed differently among various breeders and their breed standards. For example, Quarter Horses shown in halter classes could be considered overweight if judged by other breed standards. Excessive weight complicates laminitis as it increases the stress to the feet and internal structures, jeopardizing the magic balance that is basically designed for a much lighter animal.

Many horsemen think that stallions with cresty necks display more masculinity, and therefore, it is a commonly accepted management practice to allow Thoroughbred stallions to increase in bulk quickly as soon as their racing days have ended. Once they have started into the breeding program, many Thoroughbred stallions carry 200 to 400 pounds

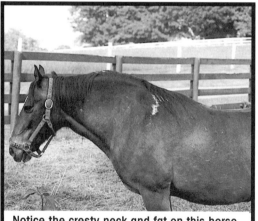

Notice the cresty neck and fat on this horse.

more than they did while in training. These horses are always at high risk. We must be careful when distinguishing between muscle mass and fat storage. Excessive weight inhibits maximum healing as it adds insult to injury.

Unfortunately, the mindset that accepts excessively overweight horses as being ideal, healthy, and a sign of good management is a real killer worldwide and is the norm on many of our horse breeding farms. Many times the owner who has a huge laminitic stallion or broodmare says, "I know they're a little heavy, but they're just easy keepers..."

Once you have recognized and accepted overweight as a blinking caution light, do something about it. I often hear my clients say they do not want to be mean to their horses. The clients claim they can tell the horses look hungry and want to eat all the time. Obesity has serious consequences for man and beast. Domesticated horses must have a controlled diet.

How do you make sure your horse gets a good balanced diet? There is a lot of very good information on today's market concerning what is right or wrong for a horse to eat. Use a reliable source to help you set your program standard and use

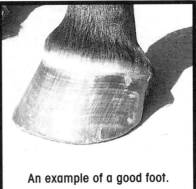

An example of a good foot.

logic. The fat horses should get less, the thin horses should get more.

Aged broodmares often become very large and carry tremendous weight due to their lack of activity, especially when they are fed an excessive amount of grain throughout the winter and are turned out in lush pastures in the spring. It is amazing the amount of weight these mares can put on in a matter of days. Being alert to each animal as an individual and attuned to their escalating weight can help you make more enlightened management decisions.

An example of a poor-quality foot.

Many broodmares' feet are in deplorable condition for various reasons. For many horse owners and breeders, the fact that these mares are used for breeding purposes only might make them ignore the condition of their feet. The mares develop toe cracks, flat feet, have practically no heels, with poor quality horn, sole bruises, abscesses, and combinations of all the above. Given a set of feet as poor as the ones described above, when these horses develop laminitis there is little natural reserve available to combat the ill effects of laminitis. Therefore, horses with deplorable feet are at very high risk when affected by even the slightest insult.

An overweight mare or stallion with very poor quality feet has little chance of surviving the significant insult of laminitis. The same horse, given a strong, durable hoof capsule, has a better prognosis for recovery.

OTHER CAUSES OF LAMENESS

There are causes of bilateral lameness other than laminitis. In some cases, bilateral lameness is often found in horses which have less than optimum foot mass and balance. Their lameness comes from one or more of several problems, including bilateral bruising, bilateral abscessing, and even marginal fractures of P 3. The signs they show for these various problems will be similar to the signs of acute laminitis. Fortunately, these problems can be treated very successfully with the same mechanical approach used for laminitis. Therefore, when in doubt, always treat for laminitis as you won't have a better opportunity than at the onset.

Many brood animals will show radiographic signs of chronic laminitis even if the mares have had no previous history of actually having suffered from laminitis. These radiographic signs can be very misleading when presented with an animal that has bilateral bruising, abscesses, or other problems due to direct trauma.

Every acute foot problem has the potential to be an emergency. Therefore, never ignore the lameness and hope that it will go away. Always treat such problems as veterinary emergencies. Call in your veterinarian and farrier for a consultation right away. Together, they can quickly determine the significance of the problem and establish a course of treatment.

CHAPTER 3

Anatomy Of The Foot

The alarm bells go off for most owners when their horses are diagnosed with laminitis. Most horse people know the syndrome is serious, but few know what actually is happening inside the horse's foot and how that foot functions.

The equine foot is made up of the coffin bone and the navicular bone and a complex network of ligaments, tendons, and circulatory system. These sensitive structures are encased by the hoof capsule, the sole, and the frog.

To help you understand the inner workings of the foot, let's review the basic anatomy. The accompanying three-dimensional schematics will make it easier to understand.

1) Coffin Bone — Pedal Bone, P 3, Third Phalanx.

Anatomy textbooks label the bone within the hoof capsule as the third phalanx, or the pedal bone. Most people call it the coffin bone. It has been referred to as the coffin bone because it lives within a protected shell, or coffin. While the hoof wall can be considered to be a protective shell, it is also a barrier. It makes a mystery of the foot because we can't see what's really happening inside the hoof wall.

The coffin bone is the last of three supporting digits and is analogous to the last digit of a human finger. It has several functions. For the purposes of this book, it serves as an anchor for the laminae that secure the hoof wall to the end of the digit. It also acts as a protective conduit, delivering the blood supply to the laminae and other growth centers of the foot. The shape of the coffin bone influences the shape of the hoof. For instance, a horse with a narrow hoof has a narrow coffin bone, while a horse with a nice, wide foot has a wide coffin bone.

The shape of both the bone and the hoof capsule is quite easily altered by environment, stress, and other factors. Wolf's Law states that bone remodels along the lines of stress. The hoof capsule does as well. The coffin bone grows and matures for the first eight to 10 years of a horse's life. The foot of a very young horse is much more easily changed than that of an older, more mature animal. This is important to know because the bone grows by ossification of cartilage along the wings and there is a large scale of normal development that is often mistaken for pathology.

Along the top margin of the coffin bone there is a very flexible cartilage known as the lateral cartilage which creates the shape of the top of the foot and bulbs of the heel. The lateral cartilage can be palpated quite easily just above the coronary band

> ## AT A GLANCE
>
> - The coffin bone is the last of three supporting digits and is analogous to the last digit of a human finger.
>
> - The coffin bone is not designed to support a direct load. It is suspended by the laminae and supported by the sole.
>
> - The hoof capsule, sole, and frog are made of modified skin cells.
>
> - The digital artery and vein serve the foot.

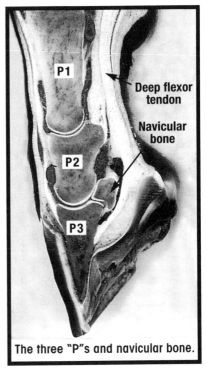

The three "P"s and navicular bone.

from the center of the foot to the heel. The portion of the cartilage that lies below the coronary band has lamellar attachment, much like that of the bone. A very young horse has very little coffin bone surface in relationship to its hoof capsule. Therefore, it relies upon the lamellar attachment of lateral cartilage to hoof capsule for structural stability.

The coffin bone is not designed to support a direct load. In a healthy foot, it functions properly when it is suspended by the laminae and supported by a healthy sole and digital cushion.

2) The second phalanx, or P 2, is referred to by horsemen as the short pastern. It sits directly above P 3 and is attached by a very strong collateral ligament support system that allows P 3 to move in an arc as the horse flexes its foot.

3) The navicular bone lies at the posterior junction to the rear of P 2 and P 3. It actually forms the back of this very intricate joint. It articulates with P 2 as well as P 3. Suspensory ligaments attach it to P 2 and another ligament attaches it to the coffin bone.

In a healthy foot, the function of the navicular bone is to support and dissipate a tremendous amount of the load forces involved as the horse's weight bears down on a single foot. It also directs the tendon attachment to P 3 and cushions the stress of the deep flexor tendon as it courses across bone when under full load.

The navicular bursa is a fluid-filled sac that lies between the deep flexor tendon and the navicular bone. The bursa supplies a lubricant in this high-stress area to protect the surfaces of the tendon and bone.

4) The first phalanx, P 1, called the long pastern, lies between the cannon bone and P 2, forming the lower segment of the fetlock joint. It is attached also by a very complex collateral ligament structure to the proximal sesamoid bones and their supporting ligaments.

The angle of attachment to the fetlock (ankle) is influenced by genetics, injury, disease, shoeing, and environmental problems. Some horses have very upright pasterns, others have short pasterns or overly long pasterns. Some horses have pasterns with exaggerated sloping. The linear alignment of P 1, P 2, and P 3 forms a very important structural reference of balance. Conformation, injuries, and diseases affecting the shape of the foot will influence this alignment.

The pastern axis is sometimes described as having broken forward, or broken back. It's easy to see how important this alignment would be as a broken forward axis transfers excessive stress and load to the front part of the coffin bone. A broken back axis transfers tremendous stress to the posterior parts of the foot, especially on the navicular bone and the ligaments attached to it.

5) The hoof capsule consists of everything you can see below the coronary band. It can be broken down into several areas: the horn wall, which goes from heel to heel and wraps around the front of the foot; the sole, or bottom of the foot; and the frog which is a V-shaped structure protruding from the sole and is attached to the bulbs of the heel.

The authors of many veterinary anatomy texts remind students that the hoof capsule, sole, and frog are made of modified skin cells. As the cells thicken and harden, they are "cornified." All such structures are non-sensitive in nature as they consist of cornified epithelial cells that have migrated from corresponding growth centers. The inflammation and reduction in blood flow that accompanies laminitis affects the growth of the hoof, sole, and frog. The sole corium is the

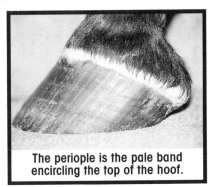

The periople is the pale band encircling the top of the hoof.

sensitive growth center for the sole. The sensitive frog is the growth center for the frog. The horn wall grows downward from the coronary groove as well as outward from the secondary laminae.

The periople is a small area that protects the coronary band. If your horse has been out in a pasture through a period of rainy weather, the periople will be easier to see, because on a foot with a high water content the coronary band becomes swollen and has a white color. As the foot dries out, the periople can be seen running approximately one-third to halfway down the wall as a thin, almost transparent membrane with a thicker, denser appearance close to the bulbs of the heel.

Many times the periople is mistakenly referred to as the shiny natural protective surface that covers the entire hoof wall. Farriers are often chastised erroneously for rasping off the shiny finish from the wall. The naturally polished appearance found on many horses' feet is actually stratum tectoreum, which is a very dense zone of horn tubules that runs from the coronary band to the ground surface.

The outermost layer of the hoof is made up of tubules held together by a matrix. They are oriented vertically. Horn wall has three zones: stratum tectoreum, stratum medium, and stratum internum. Stratum medium is non-pigmented and is normally a whitish color. The tubules that grow from the coronary band are scattered sparsely throughout stratum medium as compared to the outer layer. Stratum internum cells become the attachments for the epithelial side of the laminae.

The horny tubules actually grow downward from the coronary groove from sensitive papillae. These cells are cornified and form the

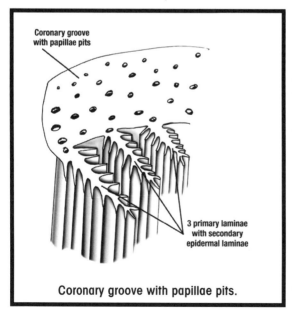

Coronary groove
with papillae pits

3 primary laminae
with secondary
epidermal laminae

Coronary groove with papillae pits.

horn wall of the hoof. Each papilla grows one tubule, taking approximately one year for the tubule to grow from the coronary band to the bottom of the foot. The matrix (a cementing substance between the tubules) that surrounds the tubules is also cornified tissue that grows from the secondary laminae, forming a network with the tubules.

The sole protects the sensitive sole, which houses the blood supply and nerves that lie between the sole and the coffin bone. It also functions as part of the back-up support group for digital suspension. The natural arch or cup is a structural roof, so to speak, that offers lift or support to the digit. This cup is naturally filled with ground surface material. My treatment will include using the cupped shape of the sole early in the syndrome and filling it with a resilient material that assists the supporting structures.

Once the sole sags, the mechanical advantages become minimal. Therefore, it is only logical that a thick, tough sole offers tremendous support and protection to the horse.

The sole is attached to the wall by a zone referred to as the white line. The term white line is misleading because this line is actually yellow and lies inside the naturally white zone of the wall known as the stratum medium. Horsemen as well as professionals routinely refer to the white line when they are speaking of the white zone. So from this point on, I will refer to this anatomical zone as the yellow line. This zone is constantly growing and maturing at the same speed as the sole. This zone is actually formed as the laminae reach their maximum growth length and become cornified. Therefore, it can be referred to as terminal laminae.

The frog functions to protect the sensitive frog from which it grows, the digital cushion, the deep flexor tendon, the navicular bursa, the navicular bone, and the intricate coffin joint. It also functions as an energy sink due to its very elastic yet durable make up. The shape is much like a wedge that functions to hold the heels apart. It is often referred to as the pump of the foot and this has been a misnomer for many,

many years. It is common to see very healthy bare feet with the frog on the ground. It's also very common to find very healthy normal feet where the frog does not touch the ground in any fashion unless the horse is on a soft surface.

Recent research by Dr. Robert Bowker of Michigan State University indicates that the frog is not the major energy sink of the foot, but rather the lateral cartilage may house an intricate hydraulic system designed to dissipate energy and heat. The bulbs of the heel join the skin to the frog and the wall. They also protect the digital cushion and are very flexible yet tough in nature due to the cornified exterior.

The function of all these cornified structures is greatly influenced by water content. A high water content compromises the integrity and stiffness of this protective shell. Healthy feet must have a tough, dense protective hoof capsule. A very low water content can result in very hard, brittle feet. Many horsemen believe a healthy foot should be a soft foot as a rule. Unfortunately, this misconception leads to many pathological problems that are simply man-made.

6) Dermal laminae: The dermal laminae are found on the sensitive vascular side of the Velcro-like attachment to the hoof wall. The dermal laminae supply nutrients to the cornifying cells and adjacent epidermal laminae, or non-sensitive laminae. They also function to attach the bone securely to its interlocking epidermal member. This area has great flexibility, but has its limits. Evidence of lamellar stress can often be seen as hemorrhage within the yellow line on the bottom of the foot. Many times this is referred to as bruising of the sole, but actually it is hemorrhage that has leached downward from previously traumatized laminae.

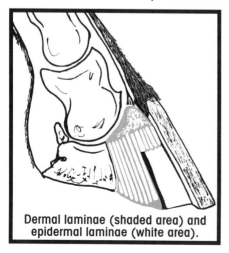

Dermal laminae (shaded area) and epidermal laminae (white area).

The dermal laminae also include the fibrous connective tissue that is the basic support for this highly vascular area. It is this zone that is involved in the very onset of laminitis. It is this zone that becomes inflamed. As it begins to swell, then becomes ischemic (causing cell death), pressures begin to build between the bone and wall because neither can expand. This sets off a very vicious cycle.

7) The circulation system throughout the foot can be separated into four basic areas. All are served by the digital artery and vein that come down the back of the pastern just off the edge of the deep flexor tendon. It is this area that you can easily palpate to find the digital pulse. The heel of the foot receives a very direct supply from the digital artery. This area is basically void of laminae and therefore remains quite healthy even in most devastating cases of laminitis. Since many people feel that if the heel is healthy, the rest of the foot will soon follow, this misconception frequently interferes with an accurate assessment of complicated laminitis cases.

The coffin bone is nourished by an artery that travels through

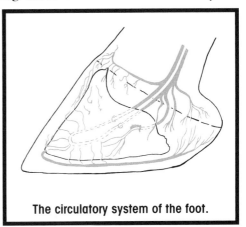

The circulatory system of the foot.

the bony canal known as the terminal arch as well as a smaller branch that runs along the exterior of the bone. The terminal arch is a major nutrient supply to the digit. In devastating cases of laminitis, this supply finally collapses and becomes dysfunctional. The terminal arch has branches that radiate out through the face of the coffin bone and assist in supplying nutrients to the laminae.

There are no nutrient foramena in the bottom, or ventral, surface of the coffin bone. The circumflex artery and vein travel through the sole corium just beneath the bottom of the coffin bone. These vessels also have multiple branches that run upward, supplying the lower third of the laminae. These vessels become compressed once the coffin bone begins to loosen from its mooring, which creates the secondary compressive stage of the syndrome.

The coronary plexus is a maze of arteries and veins that lie wrapped over the top of the coffin bone just inside the coronary groove. These vessels are an intricate part of the coronary band. They course downward, supplying nutrients to the upper most section of the laminae. Therefore, this large structural network that suspends the horse within his hoof capsule has several sources of blood supply that function as a group as well as separately to meet the demands put on the foot. Learning the basics of anatomy will help us better understand a treatment regime when faced with laminitis.

WHAT OCCURS WHEN LAMINITIS STRIKES

Laminitis occurs when an insult, either an injury or a disease process, triggers vascular constriction. Blood is shunted away from the small capillaries into larger vessels, bypassing much of the foot. The cells of the laminae begin to die, due to loss of nutrient supply. Soon, the Velcro-like attachments break off and their firm, internal connection to the hoof wall begins to erode. The degeneration of the laminae creates a devastating loss of equilibrium that otherwise exists within the normal, healthy foot.

Let's look at the basic mechanics, related to anatomy and function, of the foot. I often view the foot as a balanced machine put together with levers, pulleys, springs, cables, and shocks to maintain smooth-running equilibrium. This balance is crucial to support the weight of the horse because all of those strategically designed structures of the foot must work together in order to protect each other as well as the whole.

This is how that balancing act works:

The weight of the horse is transferred through the entire leg to the three digits: P 1, P 2, and P 3. The digits are well-supported with a very intricate network of ligaments, tendons, and back-up system consisting of the sole, frog, bars, and digital cushion. The tendons are the superficial and the deep flexor, and, coupled with the suspensory apparatus, serve to support the entire distal limb.

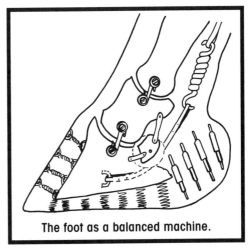

The navicular bone is secured to the coffin bone by the impar ligament, which is extremely strong and dense, and by the suspensory ligament on

The foot as a balanced machine.

the top side. The navicular bone also is a major contributing support structure. The laminae acts to suspend the coffin bone within the hoof capsule and is a critical component of the entire support system.

During a laminitis flare-up, what is happening to the feet when you see your horse literally glued to the ground? Depending on the degree of insult and duration of the syndrome, the following events occur:

The initial insult is followed by increased pulse, possibly hot feet, and an animal that obviously is in distress. Very subtle cases of laminitis may not be manifested by noticeable pain or other clinical signs. From subtle to severe cases, the intricate lamellar network is being challenged and can start to disintegrate long before clinical signs are evident, even to the well-trained eye. Several researchers have shown that the secondary laminae begin to lose shape and function hours before the first signs of lameness are present. Cell death starts in the basement membrane and quickly affects the basal cells that line the borders of the secondary laminae and act as little suction cups securing the delicate, sensitive and non-sensitive laminae. Once they have turned loose in significant numbers, a chain of events starts a very vicious cycle.

As the basal cells begin to turn loose, the laminae begin to stretch and pull apart, causing the coffin bone to rotate or

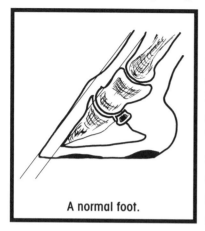

A normal foot.

sink. The weight of the horse sets heavily in the sling between the laminae and the deep flexor, resting gently against the inside of the sole and frog. Suddenly the lamellar side of the sling begins to sag, as lamellar integrity begins to fail. The tendon becomes a major force as the magic equilibrium is disrupted. When the horse is standing, its weight is placed on the laminae and the deep flexor tendon as well as other supporting structures. As the horse moves, this weight is increased proportionately to the speed of movement.

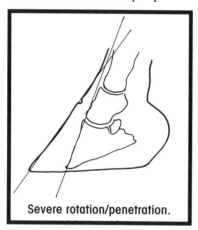

Severe rotation/penetration.

Therefore, when the laminae is inflamed, movement increases the risk of further damage. (Force walking was once advocated as a means of treating acute laminitis as movement apparently increases the blood flow and decreases the signs of pain. The down side is the risk of further tearing of the laminae. Note: Taking this risk can be career- or even life-threatening to the horse.)

Simply put, every movement enhances stress on the decaying laminae, especially turning. That's why a horse suffering from laminitis turns on its hind feet to avoid twisting the hoof capsule of the affected foot. Most horses twist their front feet to change direction of travel at the walk. This motion creates a painful response in laminitis cases. When a significant number of basal cells detach because of general lamellar dysfunction, the weight of the animal begins to tear the bone away from the mooring, creating displacement of the coffin bone. The bone is displaced along several planes.

The bone rotates away from the face of the wall, the laminae swells, pushing the bone straight back from the wall, and the bone also can sink by sliding straight down the wall.

In its normal alignment, seen in radiographs (X rays), the face of the coffin bone is parallel with the outer wall. When the coffin bone is no longer parallel to the outer wall, rotation has occurred. This happens in the majority of cases. The displacement from its normal position is seen as an angle formed by the face of the wall and the face of the coffin bone.

You may have heard a veterinarian speak of the degree of rotation. Using a set of radiographs to measure the rotation, the vet will draw a line along the face of the hoof wall. Another line goes along the face of the coffin bone. The angle formed between the two lines is an approximate measure of the angle, or degree of rotation.

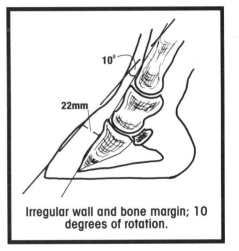

Irregular wall and bone margin; 10 degrees of rotation.

The vet must allow two to three degrees of error because the placement of the lines is a judgment call, not an absolute measurement. The reason is because the face of the wall and the face of the bone are not straight lines. Any change in displacement is very significant.

Even very small details are important when monitoring radiographic changes, but one must be very careful, as the significance of changes can only be assessed when good comparative views are taken. Consistent repeatable views are essential for success in measuring the progress of this disease syndrome.

As the tip of P 3 rotates around an arc created by the joint, the tip begins to compress the soft velvet vascular supply that lines the inner sole. The bottom of P 3 is concave, with the sharp cutting edge along its border. This cutting edge causes serious damage to the vessels and maze of nerves that supply nutrients to the sole, laminae, and bone and subsequently becomes a major source of pain. These are the compressive forces that make laminitis career- and life-threatening.

The speed of rotation depends on numerous factors, including: severity of insult, weight of the animal, lever arm forces opposing the deep flexor (toe length), exercise in the early stages, foot mass, and quality of foot. A nice, strong hoof has tremendous advantage over a weak, poor-quality foot. Horses that rotate quickly usually have more pain and a poorer prognosis than those that rotate 10 to 12 degrees over a period of six to eight weeks. Both kinds of cases can and often do have devastating results. Light-boned horses genetically bred for speed have shallow, thin-soled feet as compared to the larger-boned breeds that typically have more massive feet. All degrees of rotation within a light foot are more detrimental to its sensitive internal structures than similar degrees of rotation would be within a heavier foot.

In a typical Thoroughbred foot, a 12-degree angle of rotation will place the tip of P 3 below the ground level of the wall. Penetration is inevitable at this level. This happens less often in a heavier foot with the same degree of rotation because more sole depth exists, so the distance between the tip of the bone and the ground is greater.

Maximum compression

When I lecture on laminitis, I often make an analogy to explain the effect of compressive forces on the foot. Visualize putting your finger into a bench vice, then tightening it until it's painful. This would be akin to the very early stages of lamellar swelling and tightening against the sole corium.

Carrying through the analogy, I describe how the pain actually lessens if the finger stays in the vice. Given enough time and compressive forces, the finger will start to die due to the lack of blood flow. The pain that returns is due to the ill effects of compression and not actually the compressive forces themselves. In a laminitic horse, the degree of compression(rotation and sinking) and the duration of the compressive forces become major factors that influence the potential for recovery. I firmly believe that compression disease is the real killer, as the compressive forces shut down the circumflex vessels that supply the sole, distal tip of P 3, and lower laminae, creating a vicious cycle: more rotation means more compression. More compression forces more rotation.

The early signs of compression can be assessed with consistent, good quality, soft tissue detail, comparative radiographs. Films taken every few days can offer invaluable information concerning degree of damage and response to therapy.

Penetration

Penetration of the coffin bone through the sole simply means the sole has ruptured. Seldom does the bone itself actually protrude through the opening. Penetration appears as a tear through the sole. Through the tear you can actually see the sole corium, which is the protective covering over the bone. It is rare to see the white surface of the bone at this stage. This is a very painful stage, as there is no protection to the exposed sensitive tissue.

Unfortunately, in the past, many top show horses and racehorses have been euthanized as soon as their coffin bones have penetrated their soles because tradition has led most to believe that the condition is hopeless at this stage. Progress in

An example of a penetrated sole.

the field of equine podiatry now offers invaluable options to clients faced with euthanizing their valuable horses. A majority of penetration cases can be treated with favorable results and should no longer be considered a death sentence. Some cases can fully recover.

Long before the coffin bone has caused maximum compression of the sole, the tip of P 3 begins to soften due to lack of nutrient blood flow. The bone will start to bend — often referred to as lipping — which can be seen radiographically. These early changes are often considered insignificant, but they indicate that serious compressive damage has occurred and signals the start of bone disease. Horses that rotate 10 or 12 degrees in a matter of days normally do not show demonstrable changes in coffin bone shape.

Sinking

In addition to rotation and penetration, the coffin bone can be pushed back toward the heel, followed by sinking. This is due to the fact that the hoof capsule is very rigid and allows no room for this degree of expansive force. The coffin bone has nowhere to go but back toward the heel. This sign can be detected radiographically very early in the syndrome. Once the laminae have swollen to twice their normal thickness, the coffin bone actually starts to migrate straight down. In a worst case scenario, the coffin bone will sink two centimeters, crushing the sole corium and circumflex vessels that supply the distal laminae, sensitive sole, and distal zone of the coffin bone. Note: no sole, no blood.

With this degree of sinking, the major blood supply to the coffin bone which travels through the distal arch is often disrupted. When this happens, the coffin bone begins to die, too.

A true sinker ledge can be seen radiographically as an opaque ring. This image is created by the double tissue density found as the rim of the coronary band folds beneath the coronary groove of the wall. Some horses have a noticeable ledge that is quite normal for them and can be an area of great concern when laminitis is suspected. Radiographs at the onset of the syndrome will help determine the significance of the ledge. Note: technique in taking radiographs is vital to see it. With a normal finding, there will not be double tissue density that is revealed with true sinking. But this ledgy conformation can be very troubling when laminitis is suspected. Caution is advised in evaluating the coronary band.

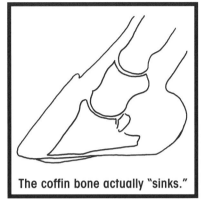

The coffin bone actually "sinks."

With both rotation and sinking, the sole can lose its cup shape. With a rotating coffin bone, the sole bulges in front of the point of the frog. With sinkers, the entire sole bulges, creating a perfect imprint of P 3. The horn-lamellar zone that can be measured radiographically is located between the most outer face of the wall and the face of the coffin bone.

Taking measurements perpendicular to either of these surfaces on radiographs will give your vet the radiographic thickness of the wall and the sensitive laminae. This dimension is normally found to be 15 to 17 millimeters (mm) in a majority of light-breed horses. In heavy broodmares, stallions and Standardbreds, the measurements will often run 20 to 21mm. Apparently there is a breed predisposition as well as an age and weight influence on the laminae and wall.

Notice the ledge: classic sinker.

It is important to know the norm for your horse. Annual radiographic exams will establish invaluable base line views that clearly define the normal quality and unique features of each foot. Remember that your horse's feet are constantly changing with age, weight gain, and changes to its environ-

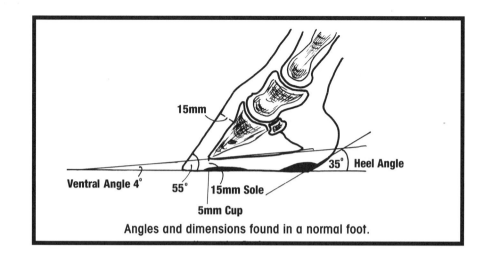

Angles and dimensions found in a normal foot.

ment. Stay abreast of the changes. This information can save your horse's life.

As soon as laminitis is suspected, your veterinarian will take radiographs on the initial examination in order to establish a starting base line. To radiograph the horse five to six days later and find several degrees rotation does not mean that it has occurred with this particular episode. If significant displacement has occurred during the first few days, your horse is in serious trouble, but if chronic rotation has been present for years and the horse has been asymptomatic, the syndrome might not be as devastating.

In nearly all cases of chronic laminitis, the hoof capsule becomes distorted. This occurs because of abnormal tendon pull and loss of counter pull by the laminae. Growth centers are distorted due to abnormal pressure, displacement, and altered blood flow.

This distortion becomes worse if the compressive forces are not successfully addressed in the treatment protocol. It is the compressive forces at work (basically all influenced by deep flexor pull) that cause the distorted hoof capsule which is the most easily spotted sign indicating chronic laminitis.

Having a full knowledge of anatomy, function, growth centers, and forces at play offers veterinarians and farriers tremendous insight and better treatment options.

Compressive forces preclude sole growth, most likely due to a diminished loss of necessary nutrients. Compressing the sole corium can occur from the external ground forces that may include a shoe set tightly against the sole. These forces are paramount in the minds of most farriers and veterinarians, and there are a multitude of mechanical solutions available to reduce or totally alleviate such compression problems. Most

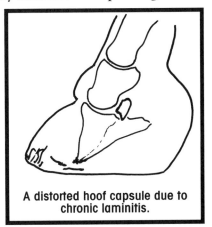

A distorted hoof capsule due to chronic laminitis.

damaging, though, are the internal forces of the cutting edge of P 3, having pulled very tightly against the inner sole (i.e. the weight of the horse as it rests against the deep flexor tendon).

Remember the analogy I used to describe the weight of the horse bearing down on the foot as a heavy load resting in a hammock.

Hopefully, up to this point, I have led you along a basic "what makes it tick" journey, giving you a clear picture of the forces at play inside the laminitic horse's foot. When I'm feeling particularly imaginative, I can actually see a tiny version of myself sitting within the hoof, making lightning fast assessments of all the forces, then formulating a plan of attack to offset the damaging forces, while keeping in mind that there are drawbacks for each of my treatment options. One goal is paramount: to return the foot to as close to equilibrium as possible, as quickly as possible.

CHAPTER 4

Treating The Laminitic Horse

CHOOSE A TEAM

The first step in treating a laminitic case successfully is to select a veterinarian and farrier who have years of good experience treating very difficult cases along with an up-to-date knowledge of the latest research and treatment techniques. Let's start with their basic qualifications, in order to explain the roles these professionals play.

All veterinarians are rigorously trained in the field of veterinary science for four to five years. At the end of this period, they must successfully complete an in-depth examination that qualifies them to practice veterinary medicine. Bear in mind, all veterinarians are trained to make a diagnosis, formulate a working protocol, and develop a prognosis for numerous species, including small animals, cats, dogs, and other companion species, large animals, cattle, hogs, chickens, turkeys, and horses. They also are trained to treat exotic birds and animals. The veterinary curriculum is very intense on the basics of veterinary science. Tissue response to disease and injury, anatomy, physiology, function, radiology, and pharmacology are taught and reinforced by hands-on experience during veterinary schooling.

Today's veterinarians have a sea of technology at their fingertips that enables them to focus on specific species and disease entities. To become highly efficient in their field, they must gain good experience and develop these skills using today's state of the art concepts and techniques. Being focused on foot problems is not always high on the list.

Your farrier, on the other hand, has learned the trade either by self training, working as an apprentice, or by a short introduction to the principles of farriery offered at private schools. The length of such programs ranges from two weeks to one year in the United States. Regardless of educational background, your farrier must become efficient in "on the job training."

> ## AT A GLANCE
>
> • Laminitis is always a red-alert emergency. Call your vet and farrier immediately.
>
> • Choose a team that has good past experience with laminitis.
>
> • Owners should have an up-to-date list of experts.
>
> • Assess the degree of damage and know your starting point.
>
> • Reverse the forces at play.

Why do I point out these basic facts concerning your farrier and veterinarian? Both will try their best to help you with your laminitic horse, drawing on their past experiences and knowledge of the subject to identify, classify the damage, and formulate a working plan that hopefully will offer favorable results. The chances that your regular veterinarian and farrier have good experience dealing with complicated laminitis cases are very slim. Why? Most farriers are focused on normal feet throughout their career. From foals to top level speed and performance horses, there is an ideal image of acceptance that they strive for with each trim or shoeing job. Depending on the breed and gait of the horses they usually shoe, many farriers become very efficient manipulating the delicate balance of the foot to enhance soundness and gait, and most learn to help the horse compensate for the ill effects of poor conformation.

Given 10 to 15 years of extensive, good experience working under the watchful eye of reputable horsemen and hopefully a master farrier, the farrier's job finally becomes

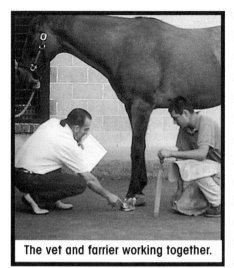

The vet and farrier working together.

merely complicated, not impossible. The more we focus on detail, the more options we have to offer. The top farriers of your area might have little, if any, exposure to complicated pathological cases, such as laminitis, serious lacerations, and other complicated disease syndromes. Many have never worked closely with a veterinarian who has developed a thorough background in the field of equine podiatry and, therefore, have not developed an eye for radiographs and other clinical data that can enhance their ability to help your horse in such a trying time.

Your local veterinarian has studied diligently to offer you the best animal health care, but most likely, has no prior experience in the field of farriery. Suddenly both well-respected individuals are brought together to treat your horse, who is suffering from an acute case of laminitis. At best, it has a career-threatening disease and the horse might be fighting for its life.

A question I often ask veterinarians and farriers as I lecture is, "How many really enjoy working on laminitis cases?" Less than 5% will ease their hands up, with far more farriers than veterinarians. It is human nature to shy away from tasks that we don't have a handle on, especially if we have been burned once. On the other hand, every one of us does exceptionally well the things we really enjoy. Stop and think what excited you the first time you rode a bicycle or swung a golf club, what pushed you to learn more about it? The very same inner feelings are vital if you want to have consistent success with laminitis. You must be on fire to make it happen and open minded so you don't get trapped in your own web.

Laminitis is a very serious disease syndrome that requires

the expertise of a well-qualified veterinarian and farrier, working closely together with common goals and sincere camaraderie. Forming such a team is the formula for consistent success. Being a farrier and veterinarian for many years has helped me understand the limitations of both professions.

THE ROLE OF THE OWNER

Become a team member from the outset. Have a serious sit-down discussion with your veterinarian and farrier concerning pertinent details, which can change the life of your laminitic horse forever. If your veterinarian and farrier examine and treat 100 laminitis cases a year and have a good success rate with the complicated cases, your horse should receive the best of care and be on the road to recovery.

My first question to owners as they call for help is, "Who is your veterinarian and farrier? Are they willing to entertain a second opinion?"

Every owner needs an up-to-date list of experts — one that puts the owner in touch with professionals from both fields who have years of good experience and a good success rate. When speaking to experienced professionals in either field, it is important to know how success is measured. We all see life differently and one person's perception of success would be failure to the next. Think of your search for laminitis experts in the same way you would think about finding a good cardiologist. If you have chest pains, it is only prudent you find a cardiologist secure enough in his or her profession that second and third opinions are considered compli-

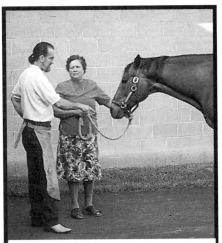
Owners should seek out experts.

mentary, instead of condemning.

An owner should be prepared for an emergency. Do dress rehearsals. Have an emergency kit prepared and ready for use (more on this at the end of the chapter). Review the basic anatomy of a horse's foot, its function, and the reasons why laminitis occurs, so that you are familiar with the syndrome.

What should you do if you suspect your horse has laminitis?

Let's look at a training horse, at its peak. Suddenly it looks like its feet have been glued to the ground. It was absolutely perfect for morning workout, but by 4 p.m. the signs of laminitis are clear. Do not panic — stop for a couple of minutes and study your horse. What is it telling you? Where does it hurt? Once you have determined what the basic message is, call your veterinarian and farrier. This is an emergency. Let them both know you are very concerned and would like to see them as soon as possible.

Since time is so critical at the outset of the laminitis syndrome, try to figure out how quickly the problem has developed. When was the last time you or another caretaker had seen the horse? Establishing the last time it was seen to be normal is crucial. How lame is the horse? Grade I to grade IV? Check the horse's pulse before asking the horse to move. Can you gauge how the pulse feels in each of the four feet? Is it faint, fine, or bounding?

Pulse and respiration: Check both before and after asking the horse to move. These parameters are very helpful, as they help define the urgency of the visit.

BUTE RECOMMENDED

If your veterinarian's office is nearby, just wait. If it will take an hour or more for the veterinarian to arrive, ease your horse's pain by giving it four grams of Phenylbutazone, intravenously or orally. Bute, as it is commonly called, acts to control the inflammatory phase of the syndrome.

Bute is sometimes erroneously referred to as a pain killer. This drug is one of the most potent products on the market.

It is used as a means to reduce inflammation and subsequently control pain and is invaluable in the early stage of the syndrome. Like most drugs, Bute can have ill side effects of which you must be aware. A note of caution: unless you are proficient with intravenous injections, do not

A low dose of Bute is recommended.

attempt this method of medicating your horse. Instead, give Bute in the oral form. Bute that gets outside the vein often causes serious complications.

STALL REST A MUST

Do not force the horse to move or exercise. Strict stall rest is crucial. For years, it was commonly thought that forcing the laminitic horse to walk would ease its pain and improve the syndrome. Although increasing the circulation in the laminitic foot can provide temporary relief, it can cause long-term damage. Movement will further harm already distressed laminae and possibly provoke rotation of the coffin bone.

What about water therapy? Hot or cold? They both work to relieve inflammation. Gauging how effective either treatment might be is related to duration of syndrome and degree of insult. I have used both with reasonable success — remember my first mare who I tied in the pond — but I no longer ad-

Keep the horse in its stall.

vocate either one, because the positive effects are often offset by the ill effects of producing a water-saturated hoof capsule that quickly loses its natural stiffness and structural function.

RADIOGRAPHS PROVIDE THE KEY

Baseline radiographs taken at the first examination will become invaluable if the case becomes the least bit complicated. Horses experiencing severe pain are difficult to radiograph. If they would rather lie down, the veterinarian will want to take the film while the horse is down. Do not use nerve blocks for the sake of taking radiographs.

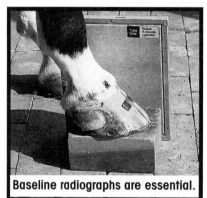

Baseline radiographs are essential.

Pure lateral views are a must for comparative follow-up films. Soft tissue detail is also a must to assess the damage properly. The soft tissue structures must be easily read. There is a tendency for most radiographs of the foot to be quite dark (over exposed). Soft tissue detail must be assessed; all increments are taken as if the bone was a silhouette inside the silhouette of the hoof. We are concerned about this relationship and how the hoof capsule relates to the ground surface.

Acute first-time cases normally will have no pathological changes on the first film unless they have Pre-existing lesions. I recommend taking radiographs every five to 10 days. Take the radiographs in the stall, or just outside the stall if necessary. Refrain from moving the horse.

DRUGS: USE CAUTION

What about all the drugs you hear about? The following drugs are often prescribed to treat laminitis: Trental, Isoxsuprine, Insulin, Acepromazine, Nitro-Glycerin cream and patches, even corticosteroids can be found in the literature as a helpful aid. Corticosteroids have tremendous anti-inflammatory action, but also serious ill effects can be experienced as well. Banamine (Flunixin) is a potent analgesic that has good therapeutic action and is frequently used the first few hours or days from onset. I find using it in conjunction with Bute can offer good results.

I used to prescribe Acepromazine, using it as a means to aid digital perfusion. Therapeutically, it is indicated, but we do not have scientific studies to confirm this concept with the laminitic horse. Therefore, I have discontinued its use as the drug reduces the alertness level of the animal, does not have analgesic properties, and makes it more difficult to monitor clinical response to Bute and mechanics.

Nitroglycerin cream as well as patches are advocated as being an aid to digital perfusion. Clinical studies do not confirm the efficacy of this drug with a reasonable number of laminitic horses and I personally have not experienced the reported success of other practitioners. Therefore, it is not part of my treatment regime. If you choose to use this product, please do so with caution, as it is a potent cardiac stimulant and can be harmful to you.

REVERSING THE FORCES AT PLAY

Having treated literally thousands of cases over the past 25 years, I firmly believe that carefully re-adjusting the mechanics of the foot provides 90% of the effective treatment. All the pharmaceuticals put together consist of about 10% of the treatment at best, especially with severe cases. I have concluded that three principles can reverse the forces at play in a laminitic foot. They are to reduce breakover, to elevate the heels, and to provide arch support.

1) Reduce breakover

Clients often ask me, "Just what is breakover?" Simply put, it is the last point of ground contact that resists the weight of the horse as the foot leaves the ground. On a barefoot horse, the most forward area of the toe that touches the ground when standing would be the breakover point. On shod horses, the point of breakover would depend on the anatomy of the horse's foot and shape of the shoe. It is the part of the shoe to leave the ground last as the horse moves forward.

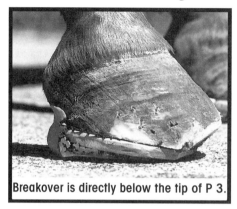

Breakover is directly below the tip of P 3.

I look at the mechanics of breakover in two ways: capsular and digital. The capsular point of breakover is where the toe breaks forward. When the foot is shod, breakover occurs where the shoe breaks forward.

The digital breakover point is much more stationary or permanent than capsular breakover, which is influenced by hoof wear, trimming, and shoeing. The horse constantly reads the point of digital breakover as it is the point that separates the lamellar pull on the hoof side and the tendon pull at its ventral, posterior attachment (the tip of P 3).

Picture the point in a simple, mechanical way. The coffin bone is like a hammock, with one side attached to the tendon, the other to the laminae, and the sole acting as a trampoline directly beneath the hammock. The weight of the horse is supported by these three entities — tendon, laminae, and sole — which are designed to meet the needs of the particular animal.

The distance between the digital breakover and capsular breakover acts as a lever that plays an intricate role in balance. Feral or wild horses have a self-correcting mechanism that regulates lever length (toe length) as it relates to the laminae and tendon pull and sole support. Domestic horses have the same genetically engineered regulating mechanism, but man regulates toe length for the horse.

A normal, healthy foot — even one with a long toe — can withstand the lever forces caused by the forward movement of the horse. But these lever forces can mean trouble for the diseased or weak foot. That's because the weight of the horse increases the pull of the deep flexor tendon, which in turn can cause tearing of the laminae. Simple 101 Physics. The laminae begin to tear and die.

Reducing capsular breakover and placing it directly beneath digital breakover immediately releases stress on the coffin bone, laminae, and tendon. Where does the load go? To the other supporting structures of the foot: the sole, frog, bars, digital cushion, and supporting ligaments.

Once again, know your starting point. The conformation of the foot and general characteristics play a big role in the degree of relief obtained by significantly reducing breakover.

Looking at the bare foot from a farrier's view, the ideal point of breakover for a laminitic case would be three-quarters of an inch forward of the apex of the frog. More on achieving this ideal later.

2) Raise the heel

Raising the heel with wedge devices releases the pull on the deep flexor and all related structures mentioned previously. By reducing the pull, the coffin bone will begin to stabilize and act as an aid to prevent further lamellar damage. The tension on the deep flexor is determined by tendon length, muscle contraction, and resisting forces forward of the digital point of rotation. All of these are influenced by the sheer weight of the animal as its internal structures of the foot sit in a hammock-like sling, made by the tendon and laminae.

Backing the breakover up reduces the forces at play that are generated by toe length. The farrier also must deal with forces directly related to tendon length. Think of the navicular bone as a mechanical pivot point, which in reality it is. One of its functions is to reduce friction to tendon and coffin joint as the tendon courses over it, much like a pulley would work in a machine. Raising the heel increases the angle of tendon insertion, therefore shortening the distance between origin of tendon and insertion.

It will help the horse if the farrier has a clear idea of what angle the horse's foot was when healthy. Very low hoof angles of 40 to 50 degrees require more heel lift than a 60- to 65-degree foot, to give the equivalent mechanical advantage. At the University of Kentucky's Gluck Equine Research Center, scientific studies were performed on experimental models with 55-degree hoof angles and concluded that up to a 70% reduction of tendon pull was obtained, with 23-degree heel wedges. Reduction of 70% is significant and can drastically reduce the damaging forces that precipitate rotation of P 3. This degree of tendon reduction was obtained without altering breakover.

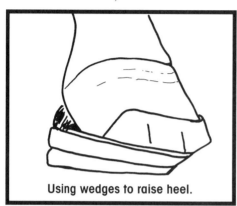
Using wedges to raise heel.

One may ask, why not raise all laminitic cases to this equivalent angle? This degree of elevation provides adequate protection to the dying laminae and unloads the sole corium, but unfortunately, severely overloads the heels. Horses with exceptionally strong, healthy heels survive the drastic shift of load to the heels, but those with crushed digital cushion, long toe, low heel conformation already have compromised heel circulation and do not fare as well, as they do not have the backup.

Using the advantages gained by significantly reducing breakover allows us to use less heel elevation and reduce

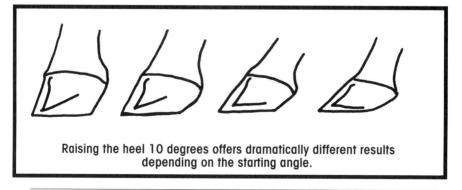
Raising the heel 10 degrees offers dramatically different results depending on the starting angle.

the side effects of excessive heel loading. This combination also allows the horse to choose where there is a happy medium. The closer we get with each case the more success we find. The long toe, long breakover cases with a toe grab have no choice — the tendon is tight and the heel is loaded, creating stress on the laminae and heel. A heel with 23-degree elevation does not have a choice either. The horse must load the heel, whether it feels good or not.

3) Provide arch support

The air space found under the foot, as a horse stands on a hard, firm surface, can be considered the arch. When the foot is off the ground, the space that is flush with the shoe or ground surface is a bit deeper than in full stance phase (maximum load). The digits seek the ground as the horse lands and the arch acts much like a trampoline. The faster they travel, the less arch on full load. The strength of the arch is influenced by many factors. Hoof conformation plays a major role when a horse faces laminitis. The strong upright foot with a deep, strong arch and heavy sole can resist the forces at play more than a weaker, flat foot with practically no arch at all.

The arch acts as natural lift. The more water content the hoof has, the less effective is the arch, as it creates sag. For this reason I eliminated around-the-clock soaks in the early stage of the syndrome. Hot or cold soaks can be beneficial, but the overall gain is offset by the disadvantages. The bare foot fills the natural arch with ground material and many times it is packed in tightly across the heels and sole. Regularly removing this natural arch support with a hoof pick has questionable validity, even though it is widely practiced throughout the world.

Using a resilient, custom-fit artificial composite to fill this are further reduces the stress on the diseased laminae. Caution is advised, however. Once the coffin bone has rotated or started to sink, the natural arch (whatever it was prior to

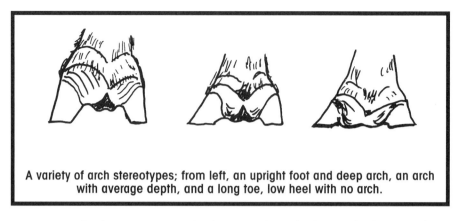

A variety of arch stereotypes; from left, an upright foot and deep arch, an arch with average depth, and a long toe, low heel with no arch.

the laminitic episode) has significantly diminished. Once the sole has reached its break level point and is sagging, it is too late to use full sole support and focus must be on supporting the structure found behind the point of the frog.

Using any and all mechanical devices requires a good working knowledge of the anatomy, physiology, and the basic function of the foot. It also requires a mechanical understanding of the forces at play and the basic options available to farriers and veterinarians. Knowing the starting point is paramount for developing a therapeutic device that has more advantages than disadvantages. The goal is to use every single mechanical option available so the summation of the positive effects will offer a more optimum healing environment for diseased laminae, compressed sole, and coffin bone.

Evaluating the effects of your mechanical devices also requires a trained eye, as circumstances are constantly changing and many times the disadvantages slowly negate the positive aspects of your device.

HOMEMADE DEVICES

In addition to the standard first aid kit, have on hand an emergency laminitis kit. Note: only experienced horse people should try using homemade devices. If possible, wait for the professionals. Your veterinarian and farrier are invaluably helpful, but roll without them if they cannot be there to help. Do not wait too long.

Your farrier can help you assemble a kit and also provide you with wedges. You also can buy wedges from a farrier supplier. Buy enough wedges to achieve an elevation of 10 to 15 degrees. If you own draft horses or horses with very big feet, you can make wedges using 2 x 6 pieces of wood. Drive nails into wood, secure the foot to the wedge, then tape over the nails.

Your kit also should contain styrofoam, plenty of screws or nails, which you will place along the toe and sides of the feet to prevent slippage, and duct tape or a similar heavy duty tape to secure the wedges.

Before applying your wooden wedge, bandage the pastern and coronary band to protect the coronary band plexus. Taping directly to the foot can shut off vital blood supply. Use the bandage as an anchor for the tape. Never tape directly to the hoof.

Have a resilient material to use between the foot and wedge, such as my Advance Cushion Support, thin styrofoam, indoor/outdoor carpet, or a plastic/rubber compound that you can buy in the craft section of a store like K-Mart. The shoes can stay on if the horse is shod. Place the foot on the wedge with a few nails or screws placed around the foot to prevent it from sliding off.

Before taping on the device, tape a piece of bailing wire along the face of the foot, fitting it to the very top of the wall and meeting the contour of the wall. This marker will become invaluable for your veterinarian, as it clearly defines the hoof wall margin, even under the bandage.

Apply the selected device to the worst foot first; wait five minutes and the opposite will be much easier to pick up.

CHAPTER 5

Shoeing The Laminitic Horse

Each case of laminitis is different. None can be treated identically. I classify the cases I treat in four categories. In the next chapter, I'll explain in detail how I assign specific grades and how treatment programs are tailored to those categories. But I want to note that in nearly all cases, I shoe laminitic horses using the three techniques I described in the previous chapter. I will now take you through the shoeing process as it is applied to particular cases.

GOOD RADIOGRAPHS ARE ESSENTIAL

First, good, soft tissue, true lateral radiographs are essential for the veterinarian to determine the severity of the case and for the farrier to shoe the laminitic foot properly. It is not necessary to pull the horse's shoes for the first series of radiographs, since they are lateral views. Actually, shod feet can offer valuable information concerning breakover and load zones. Pulling shoes on a grade III or IV lame horse can be very painful for the horse (and for the farrier, too). In many cases, it is less painful for the horse if films are made after application of mechanical aids.

Once the base line films are made, the farrier and veterinarian can discuss the details concerning the starting point. Being focused on particular characteristics of the feet, externally as well as radiographic signs of tissue damage, helps them develop a meaningful treatment protocol for each foot. Working together, the veterinarian and farrier can design a therapeutic shoe that meets the demands.

What are the demands? To reverse the forces at play. Accurately classifying the degree of damage and stage of the syndrome helps us focus on the needs of each case and each foot.

Using a nerve block on one or more of the feet might be necessary for the farrier to shoe the horse. Patient comfort, as well as safe working conditions for the farrier, is paramount. It is extremely dangerous for the farrier to work on a very lame horse, and it can put the horse through further torment.

We must remember, though, there are pros and cons to blocking. A horse that has been blocked will stand very quietly, offering the farrier the opportunity to study the foot and to trim and apply the shoe of choice. Standing on a desensitized foot, however, can cause irreparable damage. Therefore, it is wise to use a temporary heel wedge on the opposite foot to prevent lamellar tearing. I like to minimize the time I have a foot up to reduce the risk of causing further damage. Once the shoeing job is finished and the horse is returned to the stall, I strongly recommend tying the horse up for an hour or so until the block wears off. An overly active horse moving on desensitized feet can cause very serious damage to the weakened laminae.

To make this section meaningful, we must describe the case as the various categories have quite different mechanical demands. The basic mechanical formula remains constant, but the way we efficiently use it varies greatly.

CASE # 1

This is an acute case, grade III lame a few hours from onset. There are no pre-existing radiographic signs of rotation or sinking. This horse basically has normal feet. I will describe the use of Modified Ultimates™, which is my preference for all acute cases and point out the specific requirements that are met by this device. You can design and develop numerous variations of this emergency aid that can have the same benefits. (See addendum.)

The shoes can be left on provided they can fit within the limits of the Ultimates, which makes it much easier for the person applying the device, as well as the horse. Place a cotton bandage around the pastern and coronary band and

The Ultimates with Advance Cushion Support.

secure with Vetwrap. This will act as an anchor for the tape. Bandaging also protects the vital circulation to the foot. If the horse walks out of the Ultimates overnight, its weight is once again fully engaged and tears at the weakened laminae. Once the wedges are on, it is very important they stay on until adequate healing has occurred or another shoe applied.

Mix the Advance Cushion Support 50-50. This product is heat dependent and cures in a couple of minutes in 80-degree weather. The farrier might want to keep it cool to lengthen curing time until he or she become very familiar with it. Determining how much to use becomes easier with experience, but basically the farrier simply wants to fill the air space between the sole and top of the wedge of the Ultimate.

Make a hand-sized patty about a half-inch thick, place it in the bottom of the Ultimate, then quickly place the foot into the cuff. I like to hold the foot up, allowing the rubber to cure before setting the foot down, as this assures full arch support. When the foot is loaded before curing, you will find that a large amount of the rubber will push out the heels and toe, as the arch sinks under the weight of the horse. You must compromise, though, with very lame horses.

Use four-inch Elasticon™ to secure the Ultimates to the previously bandaged pastern. Using a figure eight several times over the shoe and up to the bandage works well. Duct tape should be avoided as it does not conform well for a figure eight and will cause unwarranted sweating in hot weather, but if that is all you have, use it.

I prefer always to apply the Ultimate to the most painful foot first, as it makes it so much easier to pick up the opposite foot. The Ultimate is designed to enhance breakover. When this wedge device is placed on most feet, radiographs will reveal breakover directly beneath digital breakover (the apex of P 3), which actually prevents the toe from being used as a lever against the tendon forces. This is a very strong principle of the device.

The Ultimate comes with two 5-degree wedges screwed together to facilitate gradual let down. The wedge reduces tendon pull by shortening the distance from the knee to the attachment under P 3. There are many variables that influence the effects gained by using the principles of reduced breakover, heel elevation, and arch support. When a foot falls

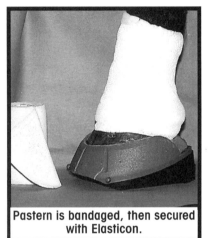

Pastern is bandaged, then secured with Elasticon.

beyond the limits of a normal range, you need to consider what modifications are needed to enhance the mechanics. Extremely long toes — with low angle (45 degrees or less) or high heels (60 degrees or greater) — require further adjustment to gain optimum effects.

When you are taping on the device, tight fit is not a concern, as the excess Advance Cushion Support will fill the space between the cuff and foot, making a snug fit. You also can glue this device on, but the cuff must fit snugly to the foot, as glue requires a thin bond membrane. I often use Equilox™ to glue on the Ultimates when there is a very irregular wall or a poor fit.

Aftercare: Use discretion; remember why the wedges are on. The laminae should not be challenged until healed or replaced and three-fourths of the hoof capsule has regrown. Rule of thumb: do not remove the wedge while the horse is on Bute. Wait at least 10 to 15 days following the last dose. If the horse is pain free, does not have a noticeable pulse, and radiographs are identical to base line films made at the onset, you can safely remove one wedge. Wait an additional 10 to 15 days and remove the last one, if all remains normal. This offers a very safe way to evaluate the degree of damage without undue risk of challenging weakened laminae, precipitating unwarranted rotation.

Cardinal rule: Do not exercise while on Bute or while using the wedges, even though the horse seems to be sounder when turned out; irreversible damage often occurs.

CASE #2

This horse has had laminitis six to eight weeks, is grade II to IV lame, and has five to 10 degrees rotation. The mechanical requirements in this case are the same as with case I, but the alignment of the digits and load zone has drastically changed. Therefore, it is too late simply to raise the heel and pull back capsular breakover.

Review the lateral radiographs. Draw a line along the base of P 3 and another along the ground plane. This forms the ventral angle, which might have started off at 10 to 14 degrees for severe club feet or at a negative angle, toe tipped up, (caudal rotation) for a foot with an extremely long toe and underrun heel. Normal angle is three to five degrees. Our goal is to shift load from the apex of P 3 to the healthy heel. Lay the straight edge along this line and draw a line parallel to it, leaving maximum foot mass. For most feet, this line would start at the apex of the frog. This is extremely important.

STEP ONE: TRIM THE FROG

Most farriers are trained to trim from toe to heel. We are

The foot above has good characteristics, such as a healthy sole, frog, and heels. The foot below is of poor quality as evidenced by its brittleness and dysfunction at the sole/wall junction.

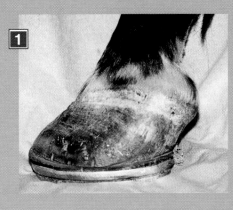

1) Chronic laminitis;
2) Chronic, complicated laminitis with draining at the coronary band (horse fully recovered after one year);
3) radiograph showing penetration;
4) radiograph showing chronic rotation.

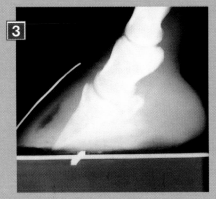

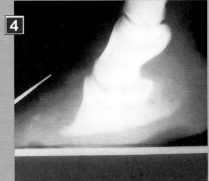

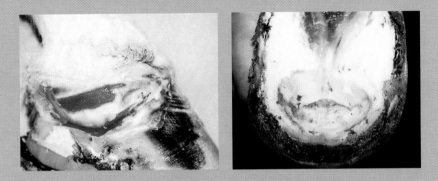

Two views of the same case: prolapsed coronary band and partial upper wall re-section (left); penetration of the coffin bone (right). Horse fully recovered in eight months.

The above, left foot shows what is called a ring of separation, which appears worse that it really is and does not threaten the overall health of the horse. The other photo shows a foot in which the coronary plexus and growth centers are destroyed, making for a grave prognosis.

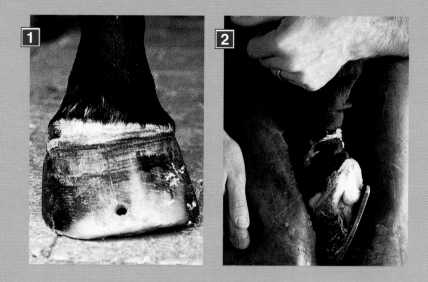

1) Sinking on one side; 2) Chronic laminitis in which the upper wall has been re-sectioned and is healing favorably; 3) Chronic, complicated laminitis with bone penetration and osteomyelitis; 4) Chronic draining track due to osteomyelitis.

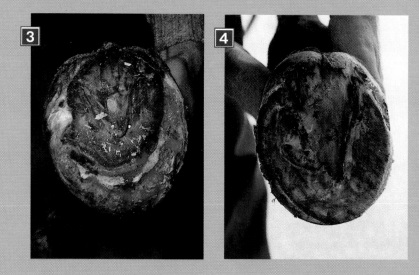

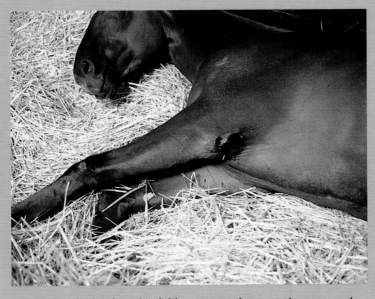

Horses suffering from laminitis can experience such severe pain that they prefer to lie down. Long periods of lying down, however, can create body sores, which look bad but are only skin deep. They heal in a matter of days or weeks once the horse begins to stand up.

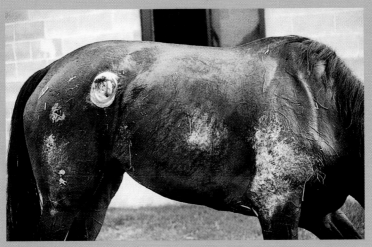

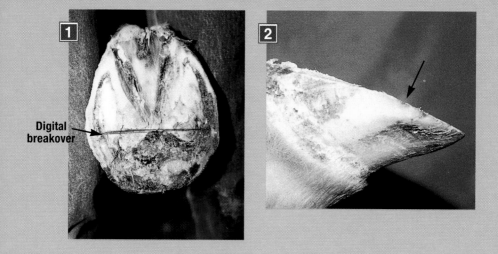

Digital breakover

Shoeing the typical high-end case with penetration

1) Derotate, reduce breakover; 2) After derotation; 3) Aluminum rail shoe.
Wide web toe protects penetrated area; 4) Measure appropriate amounts of
Advance Cushion Support. Note nails placed behind widest point of foot.

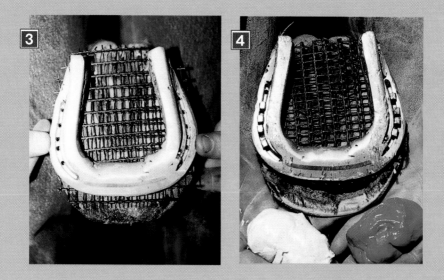

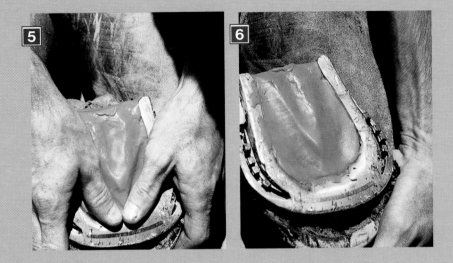

5) Mix ACS and apply to foot, filling arch; 6) Finished view of ground surface; 7) Heel view showing complete arch support; 8) Lateral view of same foot. Note breakover directly beneath coronary band.

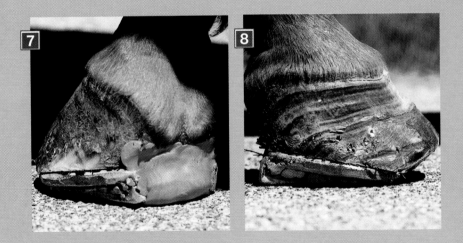

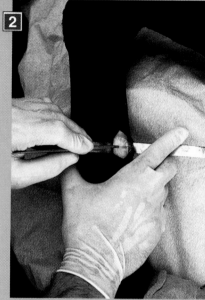

TENOTOMY

1) Mid-cannon incision along bifurcation of superficial and deep flexor tendons; 2) Cutting the deep flexor using retractors. Flexed or recumbent positioning allows the deep flexor to relax; 3) Performing a tenotomy while horse is standing and wearing three wedges. The wedges, used only during surgery, reduce pull on the deep flexor.

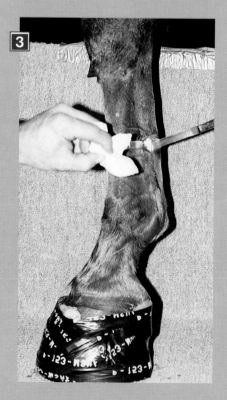

now trimming to match the ventral plane of the coffin bone, which is seen clearly on the radiographs. The only problem is we are not trimming the radiographs. The farrier must observe the foot and identify landmarks to derotate the coffin bone properly. Fortunately, we have a very consistent way to accomplish this.

Trim the base of the frog as tightly as possible. The case that is six to eight weeks from onset will have a very deep frog at the base, but it will be thinner at the apex. A case rotating 10 degrees in 10 days would not have the same distorted appearance.

Lay the rasp on the long axis of the frog. Let it sit in the shallow cup of the central sulcus and rest on the apex of the frog. This is the plane of the base of P 3 on the majority of horses. Club

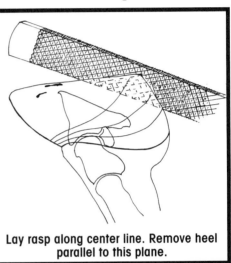

Lay rasp along center line. Remove heel parallel to this plane.

feet will be a little misleading, as their ventral angle will be three to five degrees when looking along the rasp. Observing the point at which the rasp actually emerges out of the foot tells the farrier where to stop trimming. Usually this is close to the apex of the frog or slightly behind. With excessive rotation, 10 to 15 degrees and little or no heel, this plane could be on the posterior part of the foot.

STEP TWO: TRIM THE HEEL

Having established the plane of the trim, use the rasp (no nippers) and start at the heel and work forward. Concentrate on the heels. Do not look at the toe — you are not going to use the toe in any fashion to derotate P 3. I constantly adjust the plane of the rasp to assure the heel is removed parallel to

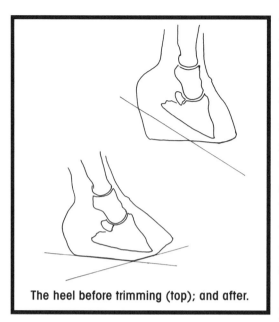

The heel before trimming (top); and after.

the plane of the freshly trimmed frog. It is not necessary to rasp down to the level of the frog, as you want to have as much heel mass as possible when finished. With shallow feet, you have little choice. I strive to push the heels back to the widest point of the frog, and often lift the toe to establish proper alignment.

Note: Accomplished experienced farriers are on auto pilot most of the time due to many years experience and will want to let the rasp go from heel to toe, developing a flat, straight plane on which to set the shoe. It is human nature to shoe foundered feet with the image in mind of the hundreds of good feet which have preceded the diseased ones. Pathological shoeing requires discipline. Be prepared for a different-looking outcome as the conditions are different. Yes, you will violate many solid standards set forth for normal trimming. This is not a normal foot and new rules must be written to meet the demands.

STEP THREE: REDUCE THE BREAKOVER

Draw a line through the long axis of the frog and another one perpendicular, 3/4 of an inch forward of the apex of the frog. This is where you want breakover on the shoe. Many ask at this point, "How is that possible when this particular foot measures 2½ inches from this selected point to the toe?" Using the rasp, rocker the toe, staying forward of the line drawn across the sole. When finished, you will have removed sufficient toe from underneath to let the foot rock forward , leaving all the sole mass you started with directly beneath P 3.

You will be tempted to take your knife and cup out the sole at this point. Don't! This is not a normal foot. This sole is very thin and you need all you can get. Take a close look at the new load plane you have established. When possible, take radiographs at this stage of the shoeing and see how you have repositioned P 3 with the ground forces.

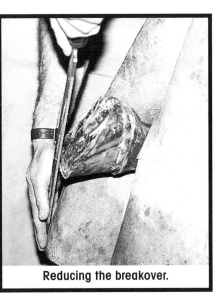
Reducing the breakover.

Having access to films before shoeing, after trimming, and after the shoe is applied offers extremely valuable information for farriers and veterinarians, allowing them to become more proficient with each foot. Farriers asked to shoe foundered horses without good, pure lateral radiographs are seriously handicapped and at best, they are looking for a miracle and a lot of luck to do the right thing. Reducing breakover requires experience, just like other aspects of shoeing.

On the first trim, the sole could be quite sensitive if the farrier is too aggressive. He or she might over-thin the sole, which is needed to protect the sensitive structures. Once it is tough and load worthy, the sole again becomes a vital, weight-bearing structure. This might be a bit contrary to traditional concepts, but I believe that most barefoot horses, regardless of the trimming techniques used, develop callused soles days after being trimmed, which helps them carry their weight more comfortably. Look closely at any bare foot that has been trimmed for at least three weeks. You will find a tough, callused portion of the sole showing evidence of weight bearing. The location of the callus and its appearance clearly indicate to me that the sole is a natural weight bearing organ.

The traditional view is just the opposite. Farriers world-wide, including myself years ago, have been led to believe that the sole must be trimmed out to allow the hoof wall to carry the load of the animal.

But a word of caution: load the sole up before it is conditioned and tough and you have a sore horse. Be patient. Remember the weight of the animal will dictate response when you remove the simple little handicaps that the horses would not have without our influence.

The mechanics of these detailed instructions are designed to unload the sole corium and laminae, offering an optimum healing environment to accelerate sole and horn growth.

STEP FOUR: DESIGN & FABRICATE THE SHOE.

I prefer aluminum for my laminitic shoes, as it is light, easy to forge, and allows me to use a very small nail. This shoe will last for several resets and is relatively inexpensive.

I use 3/4 x 1 or 1/2 x 1 aluminum bar stock for the larger feet. The stock is turned, forming a square toe. Then the toe is pulled forward. Making the toe web wide and thin toward the front edge offers a lot of needed cover and protection to the sensitive sole.

Next, forge or cut out a pair of rails determined by the degree of rotation and the amount of heel removed. Experience is a great teacher here. If the horse likes what you have applied, you probably are on the right path. I like a rail approximately a half-inch wide, shaped to meet the criteria of the shoe, running from heel to breakover. The rail sits on the inside web of the shoe and can be attached numerous ways. Three copper nails will hold it quite well. The rail can be welded on in several ways. I prefer to weld it on with a torch using an 1/8th-inch Cor-Al aluminum welding rod made by Welco. Placing the rails on the inside web enhances medial-lateral breakover and offers access for nailing.

I rocker the toe of the shoe to match the rocker placed on the toe of the foot. Note: the shoe will not touch the foot from where the rocker starts forward. Leave an air space an 1/8 inch or better. Place the shoe on the foot. You get an idea of how much Advance Cushion Support it will take to fill the arch from the frog to the ground surface. Cut a screen (provided with kit), or use gutter guard (readily found at discount and hardware stores) as reinforcement to secure the rubber and apply the shoe and Advance Cushion Support. When possible I tack the shoe on with two nails after quickly applying the rubber in two steps. The sequence is rubber, screen, shoe, and rubber.

Use a heat gun to speed up curing before sitting the foot down. I want to preserve maximum arch, then trim off any excess rubber once it is cured. Note: when placing the shoe I bring the inside web of the shoe back to the point of the frog. This assures breakover 3/4 inch in front of the frog, which is very close to digital breakover on most feet.

Aftercare: Stall rest is mandatory for the first few weeks to months. Reducing stress to diseased laminae shortens recovery time. I limit exercise until the hoof capsule is 75% replaced. Watch the growth rings. Reset every six to eight weeks, using radiographic guidelines for best results. Once the hoof capsule is regrown, most cases will show little or no evidence of rotation and have soles a full inch thick. Many do quite well barefoot and might not require shoes at all where others are shod with a four point shoe of some sort for maintenance.

CASE # 3

Chronic complicated laminitis, which can include acute rotation, penetration, or sinking of coffin bone. Horses in the upper categories use the same shoe with a slightly lower rail because they will require a deep flexor tenotomy (a procedure in which the deep flexor tendon is surgically cut) preferably immediately after derotation shoeing.

Before applying the shoe, follow the derotation and trimming steps described in Case 2. In addition, the sole/wall junction will need to be thinned and possibly opened with this case as well.

In cases of moderate to severe insult, it is important to thin the sole/wall junction. When there is apparent high-scale damage that has occurred over a few days — for example, 10 degrees of rotation or 1 centimeter of sinking of the coffin bone — it is essential to open the sole/wall junction to avoid the next stage, which will be a very painful, suppurative (pus) stage. This degree of damage will produce serum leakage that pools just under the tip of the coffin bone of P 3 and along the sole/wall junction. If the compressive forces of P 3 against the sole corium persist, then more pressure creates inflammation, more fluid, and more leakage.

Bacteria soon invades this ideal culture media and very painful sub solar abscesses are produced. The rapid-building septic condition seeks a way out along the sulcus of the frog and eventually out the heel or up along the separated laminae and out the coronary band. Each route adds pressure, which often results in a grade IV pain response.

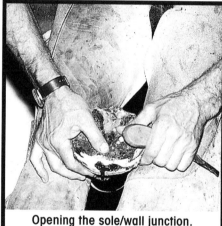

Opening the sole/wall junction.

Opening the sole/wall junction along the front edge of the hoof offers a vent that prevents or greatly retards further build up or migration of the pus. It also offers tremendous relief of pain, especially if the abscess is well established. I recommend rasping the toe off at a 45-degree angle with the ground surface until the sole is almost open from the front edge, not the bottom. Then I suggest that the farrier open the sole along its top zone. This thin membrane then will protrude just before this junction is penetrated. If it has become septic, there will be a tremendous amount of pressure behind this thin membrane.

The farrier should take a shoeing knife and very carefully open the area just above the top zone of the sole to release the pus and/or serum. Many times, the contents will be under pressure and squirt several feet when released, giving the horse immediate relief. Remember, the farrier should just open a very small slit across the front. Being too aggressive produces very painful prolapse of sole corium and granulated tissue know as Proud Flesh.

Once the sole/wall junction has been addressed, apply the aluminum rail shoe. A deep-flexor tenotomy is indicated in many cases immediately after application of the shoe. Note: not all sole/wall junctions need to be opened, only when heavy serum buildup or an abscess is present. Experience is very help here as well.

CHAPTER 6

Tailoring The Treatment

Before I begin treating the laminitic horse, I find it is essential to assign a grade to each case. Over the years, I have developed a grading system, ranging from a low of 1 to a high of 1,000. The scale is useful, because it helps to determine where the horse is in the syndrome. The scale measures the progressive pattern of the syndrome. It scores the severity of insult, response to therapy, time lapse, and even environmental influences.

Having a handle on what is actually happening to the laminitic foot at any given segment of time offers tremendous advantages concerning treatment. Simply put, when we know what is broken, we have a much better chance of fixing it. The scale helps us determine why, when, and how much, instead of just shooting from the hip with a broad spectrum treatment for all cases.

As a working veterinarian, the scale also helps me to make a prognosis. During the first few days, when the horse has acute laminitis, being able to identify the problem as a grade 900 becomes invaluable to all parties concerned. Nothing is more frustrating or demanding than unknowingly treating a difficult, high-end case, thinking everything is going to be all right, only to find the horse's foot sinking into its hoof capsule a few days later.

GRADING LAMINITIS

GRADE	SIGNS	TREATMENT	PROGNOSIS
1-250	grade I to IV lame; no rotation or sinking	Bute, wedges, arch support, digital breakover (Modified Ultimates)	very good for full recovery; recovery time 4-6 wks minimum; maximum 1 yr.
250-500	grade I to IV lame; up to 5 degrees rotation	4-point aluminum rail shoe with ACS; derotation necessary with each shoeing	good for full recovery; 6-8 mos. minimum; up to 1 yr.
500-750	grade I to IV lame; 5-10 degree rotation	4-point aluminum rail shoe with ACS; derotation essential; possible tenotomy for high-end cases; open sole/wall junction high-end cases	survival chances good; fair for riding soundness; 8 mos. to 1 yr. minimum
750-1,000	grade I to IV lame, most grade IV; many are down; 10-plus degrees rotation; all penetrated; 1 cm sinking	4-point aluminum shoe with ACS; derotation imperative, can be difficult to accomplish; immediate tenotomy; radical wall removal in cases of extensive abscessing; other options, casting using the above therapy, amputation	fair to guarded for salvage; years in recovering

GRADE 1-250

Signs/Symptoms

Up to 80% of horses with laminitis fall within this category. In most of these cases, there is not a specific reason pointing to why the horse developed laminitis. I often hear clients say, "Nothing has changed in this horse's life over the last few months. Why does he have laminitis?" Sometimes, I simply do not know.

What do they look like? These cases range from mild to very significant signs of pain. Clinically, the horses with mild damage as well as the serious cases can be quite lame, as much as grade IV.

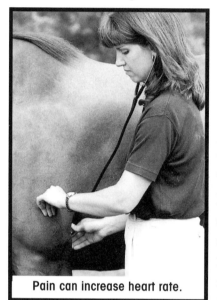

Pain can increase heart rate.

Pain is not always a dependable indicator for a laminitis scale as pain threshold usually varies greatly, just as it does with people. Obvious signs that a horse is in pain can include increased respiration and increased heart rate (know what's normal for your healthy horse and use that as a benchmark to measure any changes). Note, however, that both respiration and heart rate also are increased with excitement and exercise. When a horse's heart rate jumps up when it is asked to move or made to get up, it is a good indicator that increased pain is due to increased weight bearing and, most likely, is foot or leg pain.

Pain changes the facial expression of most horses. The eyes seem more prominent and they do not have a focused look. If anything, they appear to be looking back, veins on the face become more prominent, and nostrils flare as the heart rate jumps up. When a grade III or IV is asked to move, you can actually hear its heart throbbing from several feet away.

Many horses within this category will show obvious signs of lameness, a reluctance to move, or both. They sit back on their hind feet, transferring the weight off the front legs. When asked to turn, they shift around on the hind feet, much like a rabbit. This could be your first clue that something is dreadfully wrong.

Appearance of the Feet

The feet can appear and feel normal to your touch. However, they can feel quite warm as well. But be careful using this parameter as an indicator as many other circumstances will cause the feet to heat up. A visual examination is informative, but to feel the contours, detail, and characteristics of a particular foot is by far the best way to make an assessment. This is why the help of your farrier is so vital.

Your farrier has "eyes in every finger" and can feel very subtle changes that are often hard to see. Why is the farrier's touch perception so keen? Stop to think about an average full-time farrier who is in a trimming practice. He or she could easily trim 40 to 50 horses a day. That's 200 feet, 1,200 a week, 4,800 feet a month, or 57,000 a year. Give them 10 years in the business and they have handled half a million feet.

Sense of touch enhances the farrier's trimming and shoeing work, just as a heavy surgery schedule does for veterinarians. Farriers have developed a totally different sense of touch, as their daily exposure to the horse is quite different. Working closely together as a team, their experience and knowledge of the foot offers unlimited options. Accurately assessing the foot by eye and feel requires a good understanding of what is the range of normal.

Shallow, weak, generally poor quality feet seem to feel the effects of laminitis much more easily than strong, thick, solid feet. Excessively long toes will sting the laminae more than short, stubby toes. Excessive chipping, standing on concrete, and many other variables will influence not only the pain

Weak feet have inherent risks.

response, but the damage as well. My point is, given a certain dose of insult to measure without actually being able to view the damaged laminae means that both the farrier and the veterinarian must study the effects of the damage as it relates to the foot and horse.

How to Treat

Remember laminitis is most often a secondary syndrome following an existing injury or disease. Therefore, the veterinarian must examine and treat the whole horse as well as the feet. At the first detection of onset of laminitis, the horse should receive 4 grams of phenylbutazone, commonly referred to as Bute. A mechanical device to reduce tendon pull should be applied immediately.

Be judicious with Bute. The potent anti-inflammatory action of Bute can quickly relieve all signs of pain and successfully shut down the inflammatory state of this syndrome. You must remember that the horse is not healed yet and is far from normal at this stage even though the horse might not be exhibiting signs of pain. Therefore, you must allow proper time for the inflammation to subside, all the while providing a stress-free environment for the laminae to heal.

Lacerations, severe bruises, and other obvious injuries all heal at a set rate that you can monitor easily as you actually watch the healing process. What happens inside the laminitic feet remains a mystery as we cannot observe this process. I often hear, "He is pretty good on Bute, Doc. Why can't I go on with him?" Just stop to think about what is really happening mechanically, when a horse requires Bute or any other analgesic to diminish the effects of lamellar dysfunction.

How to Shoe

As a rule, most cases that score 1 to 250 on my scale do not require the application of a therapeutic shoe. Simply apply a Modified Ultimate Wedge™ with Advance Cushion Support™ as a first line of defense, for even with the very mildest of cases, as you cannot identify the mild case from the more severe at the onset of the laminitis syndrome.

Cases in the 1 — 250 range will not have any rotation or displacement; therefore, your farrier will not have to de-rotate the coffin bone. The farrier should elevate the heels and reduce breakover. The Modified Ultimate Wedge™ provides both. Remember that it usually takes two, five-degree wedges to build the proper angle for the first shoeing of most laminitic horses. Having several wedges in the correct sizes for your horses, or having a hand-made device that can be readily slipped on as an emergency aid, becomes incredibly valuable when you first discover one of your horses in the acute phase of the disease.

I prefer not to nail a shoe on an acute horse the first few weeks of the syndrome as it can cause further stress to the laminae. I find it always best to refrain from shipping an acutely laminitic animal long distances during the first few days or weeks of the syndrome as shipping can precipitate unwanted stress on the laminae.

Prognosis

The best scenario: 24 hours after the application of wedges, the horse is clinically normal, pulse hardly detectable, and is very active in the stall. Give it another 2 grams of Bute and observe over the next 24 hours. If the horse remains clinically normal, discontinue all medication. Leave the horse resting in its stall for 10 days. No test runs. You will be tempted to resume working your horse, especially if you are on a tight training schedule, but you will only lose valuable time.

Ask your vet to take a second set of films with the wedges on. He or she will need to be disciplined in technique to use the new films to compare to the first ones. They must be identical views if you are going to assess minute changes that might have occurred. If there are no radiographic changes and the horse has been off all medication for 10 to 15 days, it is safe to remove one wedge. Wait another 10 to 15 days and remove the second and last wedge, provided radiographs once again reveal no changes whatsoever. After removing the wedge, if the horse shows any degree of soreness when turning, put the wedges back on, resume the Bute, and start the countdown all over. The laminae simply are not ready to be challenged.

Once the wedges are removed, the farrier must address the long toe that has developed over the past 30 to 45 days. The four-point trim will reduce the tendon pull and offer an optimum healing environment for the slightly damaged laminae. A four-point trim follows the same basic principles laid out with the mechanics for treating laminitis. Capsular breakover will be approximately three-fourths to one inch in front of the apex of the frog. The heels are pushed back to approximately the widest part of the frog, which assures full heel support. The quarters are gently rubbed out, enhancing medial-lateral breakover. And the sole is left intact so it can bear weight simultaneously with the wall.

Each time the farrier trims and re-shoes the horse, he or she will remove as small an amount of horn mass as possible. Note: this is an area that many farriers have trouble learning because traditional methods call for cupping the sole out in order to prevent sole pressure. Another common error that invariably causes a sore horse is to trim the foot in a traditional fashion, then try to apply the four-point method. You simply do not have enough foot and the horse does not appreciate your effort.

With the removal of the wedges and application of a four-point trim, the horse is sound, behind schedule, and everyone is anxious to play catch up. Not yet — it's too risky. Hand walk, or walk it under saddle for an additional 15 days before resuming exercise in any fashion. Approximately 45 to 60 days will have elapsed since the first signs of laminitis. You might feel that your schedule is totally destroyed. But you can rest assured that most likely you have saved the career of your horse.

Observe the characteristics of the growth ring that has developed over the past six to eight weeks. Growth rings are quite visible to the eye and can be palpated as well. They make a concentric pattern from top to bottom around the hoof. They tell the past history of the hoof as well as overall health of the hoof and previous activity of the animal much the way the rings of growth tell the history of a tree. The rings indicate roughly a 30-day growth period compared to one year for the ring on a tree. The distance between the rings changes with the rate of growth, which is influenced by multiple factors.

A sudden burst of horn growth occurs in the spring, possibly due to the biological time clock. During colder, more dormant times of the year, the rate will decrease. The accelerated growth is seen as a raised band of horn. With the normal foot it can be as much as three-quarters to one inch in width. When slow growth occurs, the new hoof will have a more contracted appearance at the coronary

Notice contour of growth rings.

band. Sickness, high fever, stall confinement, drastic changes of environment and many other circumstances often cause a temporary shut down of horn growth.

Most rings from laminitis will appear very tight and the farther down the hoof they grow, the more prominent the old horn becomes as it is being pushed down and outward by the new growth. When there is distinct, tight new hoof growing down, consider everything below the junction of the old and new to be weak and supported only by diseased, decayed laminae, which can be seen easily along the ground surface when the foot is trimmed. With complicated cases, this dark, hemorrhagic swollen area runs up the hoof wall right to the junction of the new wall and the old. Once it has grown down the wall to the level of the bottom of P 3, it is safe for the laminae to be challenged — and not before.

Everyone asks me, "When can I turn my horse out? When can they go back in training?" The hoof's very distinct growth area is something everyone can see. It can help you monitor when the horse can return to a free exercise situation. Let's take a typical example: Your horse has responded very quickly to treatment. It has a good half-inch of new growth; a very fine growth ring appears between the new and the old, indicating a very subtle disruption of growth pattern. The horse appears 100% sound both radiographically and clinically. The horse is off all medication. Most likely the feet are back to normal and only went through the inflammatory stage of the syndrome.

Note: many experienced horsemen think all noticeable growth rings, regardless of their characteristic, indicate a foot problem. Therefore, it is common for most sale horses to have the normal rings rasped off by their farriers to prevent prospective buyers from making that assumption too. Unfortunately, this practice is very deceptive at best. In Europe, no one would think of doing this.

Another example: The ring is quite deep and very wide, leaving the new growth set in slightly from the old horn. This horse is normally three to six months away from a training schedule at best. Why? It has significant lamellar damage that simply has to be replaced. When trained, especially when speed is part of the program, this horse will have trouble. Its feet will heat up, the pulse will be stronger than normal, and it will walk tenderly on hard surface.

Horses in the upper ends of the 1 — 250 classification might require up to one full year for full recovery. I often see horses stop and go, stop and go for six to eight months and slowly reach the point of no return as athletes. Give them adequate healing time. They do not carry their feet on their back — they use them more than any other part of their anatomy. A single bad foot will stop the best horse and can cost him his life. I often tell my clients, "A sound horse can catch up in a very short time; a lame horse never does."

Horses in this category will have no measurable displacement of P 3, other than a slightly thickened laminae of 1mm to 2mm. Allowing time for the damaged laminae to be fully replaced without undue stress will eventually produce healthy, functional laminae. However, other horses in the same range on the scale can deteriorate to several degrees of rotation, first stage bone disease or higher, and have a very abnormal horn growth pattern. When the destructive forces of laminitis are not successfully addressed, a three-to-one heel-to-toe ratio is a common finding when the laminae have been tested long before it has been replaced. Apparently, the overall health of the basement membrane has a bearing on whether the laminae can heal or must be replaced.

GRADE 250 — 500

Signs/Symptoms

The horses that get into the feed overnight, the horses who have been on lush grass for several weeks and were plenty heavy when turned out, and those who have a reaction to a vaccination or medication of some sort have the typical histories in this category. There is a very distinct set of circumstances associated with laminitis cases in this part of the scale. We can't prove what has caused the laminitis, but there certainly seems to be a viable reason to explain the syndrome.

On his or her first call, the veterinarian will do a physical exam very similar to that of the cases in the 1-250 range. The results might show all parameters within normal limits except for an elevated pulse, possible warm feet, and pain response. Most will be grade II to grade IV lame.

Appearance of the Feet

Some horses in this category with chronic damage will have feet in which the heel grows faster than the toe due to lamellar damage. Radiographs will show that horses within this range typically have a few degrees of rotation, 3 to 5 degrees, within 45 to 60 days from onset and they might have up to one centimeter of sinking.

How to Treat

The treatment is identical to that described above for cases in the 1-250 range. The big difference is that horses in the 250-500 range are treated in the same way, but their response to the same mechanical treatment is much slower because the damage is greater. It may take several weeks to wean the horse off Bute, then several more weeks or months to take off the wedges or a rail shoe.

You will precipitate rotation if you are in a hurry and misjudge the degree of damage. If you first detect a problem three to four weeks after the insult occurred and no mechanical protection has been offered, the horse might have three to five degrees of rotation and require a low level of Bute for an extended period of time to return to 100% soundness. The growth rings will begin to show a slight discrepancy of toe to heel as heel growth will start to exceed toe growth. The same animal often is kept in training while on Bute and continues slowly to tear the laminae, moving the horse up the scale for damage, producing unwarranted rotation and compressive forces that eventually will destroy its career and possibly life.

How to Shoe

At this stage, before the farrier goes to work, he or she will need access to good quality radiographs in order to fine tune the realignment of P 3 (de-rotation) before applying the wedges or a similar devise offering optimum mechanics.

Three to 5 degrees of rotation is considered very mild by many and often shrugged off as being very insignificant. Unfortunately by the time it becomes evident that the horse cannot train with persistent foot soreness, the chances of full recovery are slim. Tremendous damage has altered the intricate lamellar network and precipitated further displacement of P 3. In such cases, a four-point aluminum shoe with Advance Cushion Support™ is preferred over using the temporary solution provided by the Modified Ultimate Wedge™ because it will be necessary to change the angle and breakover on the foot for several months during recovery. The shoe prevents a few maintenance problems that can be found with long-term bandaging, taping, or even attaching a wedge or shoe with glue.

Prognosis

Recovery time will be eight months to one year and often these horses step down in class, especially speed horses. Most will recover with no evidence of rotation, but will have subtle changes to the distal end of P 3. Slight lipping (bending) of the tip of P 3 indicates a significant insult has allowed sagging of the bone, causing inward compressive forces against the inner face of the sole. The tip of P 3 simply bends upward due to the unrelenting load placed on its perimeter. The bone is not designed to carry excessive load around its very thin, fragile border.

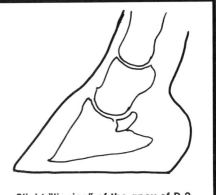

Slight "lipping" of the apex of P 3.

The circulation immediately below and along the distal face of the bone is compressed, leading to further lack of nutrients and the bone continues to soften. Slow death of bone cells sets in.

Basically when enough healing time is allowed, the entire hoof capsule and lamellar network are replaced. You have an athlete, but get in a hurry and you have only a reasonably sound turn-out horse or one that changes occupations entirely and steps down to slower sports. A lot of very nice athletes go this route, due to tight schedules and lack of knowledge of the subject. Top level horses in this category are constantly

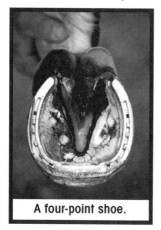

A four-point shoe.

getting into trouble. Helping them recover demands caution, patience, and a keen eye for detail.

A horse in this class might require a four-point shoe for the remainder of its athletic life to assure minimum lamellar and sole stress. No big deal. It can be fixed and returned to an acceptable sound state given time and proper mechanics. Successful treatment of this class must be thought of as literally months — not days or weeks. Impatience and the lack of basic understanding concerning normal hoof growth and mechanics cause many unwarranted problems, great frustration and tremendous economic loss with a large number of horses in this class.

GRADE 500 — 750

Signs/Symptoms

For scores in the 500-750 point range on my scale, history plays a major role when classifying this horse. Typically, the

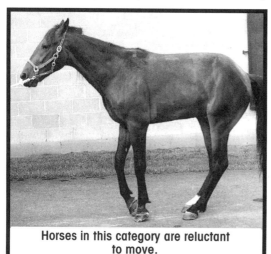

Horses in this category are reluctant to move.

horse develops laminitis after an incident such as excessive grain consumption with several hours or days lapsed before treatment, a severe bout of colic, or recent surgery, dystocia, metritis, retained placenta, corticosteroid therapy, pneumonia, pleuritis, and others.

Lameness for many of these horses will be grade

IV right from the onset. The horses must be forced to move and when they do, they go forward with a slow, very hesitant gait as if trying to walk on their hind legs. Many will lie down and be reluctant to get up. Their coronary bands will be very tender to palpate. The lower legs can have generalized edema and a large majority of the horses will have hind foot involvement, too. These animals are extremely uncomfortable, suffering great pain, and are obviously stressed. They are considered too sound to euthanize, but too lame to live, which leaves them in a deplorable state of health. If you have a similar case on your hands, hopefully the suggestions in this book will offer your horse help.

Appearance of the Feet

After several weeks or months, the hoof capsule has changed dramatically in chronic cases. The sole has bulged well below the wall. Horn growth over the surface of the hoof capsule could show a four- to-one toe-to-heel growth deficit, which causes the toe to turn up and the heel to become excessively long. The bulbs of the heel are many times higher than the wall at the coronary band.

Laminitic horses this far along the scale often have the first three stages of bone disease. Compressive forces have destroyed the blood supply to the distal apex and osteomyelitis becomes a major concern. Stage V bone disease also can be found with very long-term cases of this class. In the majority of cases, the P 3 bone will have penetrated the sole, causing pus and serum to drain continuously out the bottom of the foot as well as seeping from under the coronary band. Eventually, the entire end of P 3 will become severely

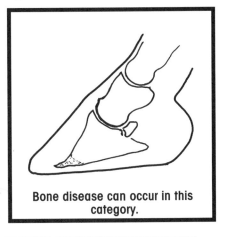

Bone disease can occur in this category.

eroded. The condition of many of these long-term, complicated cases will slowly degenerate into the final, and very grave, classification.

Radiographs will show that horses in the 500-750 point category have eight to 10 degrees rotation, with or without one centimeter of sinking, within a few weeks of the onset of the syndrome. Light-footed horses such as Thoroughbreds and Quarter Horses will normally penetrate with 12 degrees of rotation. When you examine such a horse several hours or days from onset, you might find a very palpable ledge along the coronary band that can be confirmed radiographically as evidence of sinking. This might occur along the front only, on either side, or all the way around the coronary band.

The sole might have a noticeable bulged profile that your farrier will be able to detect. All feet are slightly different, even on the same horse. Each foot on a laminitic horse will show slightly different changes in sole shape. Seldom is the damage identical from one foot to the next, even with the same horse.

Radiographs also can reveal a distinct subwall lucency from seven to 10 days from the onset of acute laminitis. Other metabolic parameters can be drastically off scale as well and must be addressed to keep this patient in a manageable category.

How to Treat

Your veterinarian and farrier must address this case together. They must have great appreciation and respect for each other's ability to sense and execute adequate therapy. Horses in this part of the scale are often seen as chronic, complicated cases. Previously, the horses might have been treated with various therapeutic shoes and pain-killing drugs. Basically, they often appear to have responded favorably to even the slightest mechanical properties offered with various shoes, techniques, etc. But unfortunately, six to eight weeks from onset, they will show an acute exacerbation of the signs once again. At this stage, owners oftentimes will make the mistaken assumption that the horses have foundered again. This is the secondary stage, or suppurative stage (see the glossary), of the syndrome. It is not a new laminitic episode. The horses' acute pain response is due to migrating infection either up the wall or under the sole. It also is associated with the early stages of bone disease.

Lamellar pain at this stage has subsided. The horses might have foul smelling pus draining from the coronary band or out around the bulbs of the heel. Even with this class of damage, most of the signs of severe displacement, soft tissue and bone damage could have been prevented or at least significantly lessened with better first-line mechanical therapy. Cases in this part of the scale are predictable and manageable provided you have accurately assessed the damage and applied proper mechanics.

Within weeks of the onset of laminitis in such a case, it becomes obvious to everyone involved that the training schedule is out and the only hope is to save the life of the animal. This is a tough realization, sending shock waves through everyone involved with caring for the animal. But don't panic - with a little luck you can still pull it through. Just simply address what's broken and let Mother Nature do the rest.

The use of Bute, Banamine, or other potent, non-steroidal anti-inflammatory drug is indicated for all such cases. Patient comfort is a major concern. I feel it aids healing animals in severe pain. Others disagree. They prefer not to treat with any drugs with direct or indirect analgesic properties. Their school of thought is that if the horse lies down, it doesn't contribute further damage to its feet. Very true, but the benefits of this approach are questionable and seldom make a significant contribution to the overall recovery of the horse.

I go to great efforts to provide a comfortable environment as well as a pain-free recovery for all my patients. I feel treating the mind of a severely injured or diseased animal plays a major role in creating conditions favorable to recovery. Keep the horses happy and content and most will heal very quickly.

Changing the feeding schedule for depressed and suffering patients has helped many of my tough cases survive mentally as their feet are slowly growing back. I feed four to six times a day. And I feed " treats," whatever a horse likes best; from home-cooked concoctions that smell delicious to peppermints, carrots, apples; whatever it takes to stimulate some interest. There is something magical about food for man and beast. We eat when we're tired, sad, depressed, sick, or inactive. Just having something in our mouths apparently releases endorphins, which give us a moment of contentment. It works. I'm not really sure why.

I have put foundered horses together in the same stall as comfort companions—- in a 17- by 17-foot box stall. I thickly bed the stalls for the ones that are down and do it in a very special way. A ring of straw bales goes around the wall and shavings are banked up over the bales followed by a deep layer of straw. This makes a nice pillow for them and they soon learn to lie along the wall with their head and neck on this elevated area in a half-sitting, half-lying position. It's much easier for them to lie down and get up as they are never lying out flat.

How to Shoe

Soft tissue pure lateral films taken at weekly intervals will offer valuable information concerning the speed and degree of deteriorating that has occurred. The farrier will shoe a horse in the 500-750 range on the scale in the same way previously described for horses who fit in the 250-500 portion of the scale. When presented with a case with more severe damage — a distorted hoof capsule and radiographic evidence of advanced bone disease — the farrier must adapt his or her techniques to meet the demands of the particular foot.

Before raising the heel to release tendon pull, the coffin bone must be realigned with the ground and upper digits.

Failing to de-rotate the coffin bone before addressing pull with wedges or doing a deep flexor tenotomy, a surgical procedure in which the tendon is cut to release pressure (see the description below), offers minimal results at best as the mechanics are just not right. The apex remains loaded due to the malposition of P3. I can't stress this point enough. That's where good experience and/or working with others who have a good success rate becomes invaluable to you, your veterinarian, and your farrier.

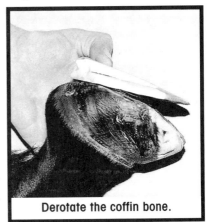

Derotate the coffin bone.

Caution is advised when re-aligning P 3 in cases with excessive rotation, penetration, or long-term chronic osteomyelitis. There are two basic ways to accomplish this. Remove heel, starting at the base of the trimmed frog, raise the toe, or do both. A light foot with a long toe and low heel conformation does not have adequate heel to remove and attempting the de-rotation with a rasp routinely creates a new painful response as valuable sole is lost and the sensitive structures of the foot are left with little or no protection.

Once I go to the nail-on shoe, I use one basic kind of shoe that meets the mechanical standards of one particular foot. I prefer an aluminum rail shoe with breakover placed directly beneath the point of digital rotation (or the apex of P 3). The rail height depends on the degree of rotation. Usually, the farrier chooses a shoe with a rail between 3/8 and 1/2 inch. The penetrated sole is protected behind the wide web toe of the shoe. Rasping the toe off at a 45-degree angle allows medication of the penetrated area from the front.

Advance Cushion Support™ is placed over the entire sole, frog, and bars and has contact with the ground surface. The mechanics of attaching a shoe this way have tremendous advantage over the glue on or taped-on wedge, as it can be securely attached to maintain normal alignment. Notice in the photograph here how the nails are placed well behind the widest point of the toe and prevent the necessary heel loading.

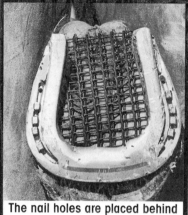

The nail holes are placed behind the widest point of the toe.

Horses in the upper range of this category often appear to show favorable results to the described shoeing technique, but " stall out," so to speak, after two or three weeks and just simply stop showing a continued favorable response clinically, as well as radiographically. They require 2 to 3 grams of Bute to be made more comfortable and to reduce the damaging inflammation. They have little or no appreciable sole growth. If the horse fails to double sole depth in 30 days and would rather be down most of the time, instead of up and alert, I suggest a deep flexor tenotomy at this time. Why so soon? For several reasons:

1) It offers the maximum healing environment for the laminae, as well as sole corium and bone. When shod properly, the stress to the laminae, bone, and inner sole is dramatically reduced as the weight of the horse is transferred to these structures via the deep flexor. Therefore, the potential for an immediate boost to circulation is enhanced.

2) The tendon heals quickly. Seven to 10 days following surgery, mid-cannon, the lower segment of tendon will become attached to the surrounding tissue and the surgically cut tendon ends are firmly bridged with fibrotic tissue in two to three months. In six to eight months, the tendon is functional and one year later fully recovered, with exception of the scar.

3) Providing a means to grow massive sole rapidly over a potentially penetrated or necrotic coffin bone prevents the

majority of higher scale bone disease seen frequently with complicated cases. By the time the foot has fully recovered, the tendon has undergone full recovery as well.

Having a horse with a high level bone disease and an intact normal deep flexor is not a desirable end goal, as it lives a miserable life as a chronic cripple. On the other hand, having a penetrated foot with an inch or more solid, durable sole, little if any evidence of bone disease, and a thick place on the tendon offers a better quality life, meeting more ideal long term goals.

Prognosis

If rotation of eight to 10 degrees occurred while the horse was wearing its normal shoes (long breakover), and it has little or no mechanical backup, the prognosis can be good for a riding sound future, as deterioration is slow. On the other hand, if rotation occurs while using maximum mechanical principles, this case slides to the next level of scale and the prognosis is guarded as insult has caused insurmountable damage to the laminae.

Goals must be set with these difficult cases, as well as the lower scale ones, but the difference is a serious commitment from all involved. Treatment is more intense, requiring the expertise of a knowledgeable farrier and veterinarian. Even this level of effort is not without the risk of losing the horse later if its condition worsens. To offer a maximum healing environment for penetrated cases or those that are at high risk of developing osteomyelitis, more aggressive action is required.

GRADE 750 -1,000

Signs/Symptoms

This category is life-threatening from the start. The majority of horses in this category have coffin bones which have penetrated their soles. Massive lamellar death can occur within hours or days of the onset of acute laminitis. These horses also have draining at the coronary band, as well as the heel, within days or weeks of the onset of the attack. The majority of such horses can become candidates for euthanasia quite early in the syndrome. For many of them, it's justifiable. Sometimes, it's the kindest thing you can do for the horse.

At the onset, their pain can range from going off the scale to virtually none, due to physiologically anesthetized feet. Starting at the low end at 750, we might see a horse with one centimeter of sinking and a few degrees of rotation on one

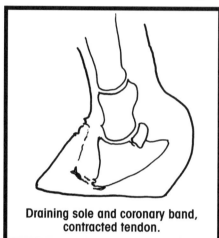

Draining sole and coronary band, contracted tendon.

foot or any combination. At the other end of the scale, a horse could have 12 to 15 degrees of acute rotation with penetration of the sole evident within the first few weeks of the syndrome.

The slower the displacement, the better the prognosis, but there is a limit to the degree of compressive forces that a horse can endure. You can only shut down the blood flow for so long; otherwise you have irreversible damage to these cells. Mechanical compressive forces can be dealt with, and the quicker the better. The chronic cases might have high level bone disease with associated severe contraction of the deep as well as superficial tendons.

You'll begin to understand the seriousness of such cases if I use the following example of a horse reaching 1,000 on the scale:

I was called in to treat a 2-year-old Thoroughbred colt. He was extremely valuable, quite healthy, and in training for racing. Following a morning gallop, he developed a fever and all four legs began to fill. Within hours he was showing signs of acute quadrilateral laminitis (involving all four feet). On a pain scale of one-to-four, his pain level would have been described as eight! Despite intense supportive therapy and potent analgesics, he remained unresponsive.

I saw the colt within 24 hours of the onset of acute laminitis. He was standing in cross ties with all four feet in a line fashion, one behind the other. He looked as if he were trying to balance on a tight rope. His eyes were dull and unfocused. His lips curled back in a grimace, and he was grinding his teeth, which could be heard several stalls away. All four feet had a noticeable ledge and were ice cold. Using a bottle of Carbocaine on each leg, I attempted to do nerve blocks on all four feet. My goal was to relieve his intense suffering and then perform a venogram on at least one foot.

By using massive doses of the blocking agent on him, he was able to walk out of the stall with great difficulty. But I still could not pick up a foot. We managed to get a venogram on one foot, which proved to be very risky for me and my associates, because the colt had no comprehension of what he was doing. He was blind with pain. The venogram revealed no contrast at the coronary plexus, down the front of P 3, along the vertical surface, and through the terminal arch. Contrast was present only in the bulb of the heels. There is no way to help a horse with such massive damage.

The colt had to be euthanized because he was suffering so horribly with no hope of recovery.

Appearance of the Feet

There are usually noticeable changes in the feet with horses in the acute stage of this category. Chronic laminitis cases in the 900-point range have extremely dysfunctional feet, advanced stages of bone disease, chronic draining tracks, and excessive contracted

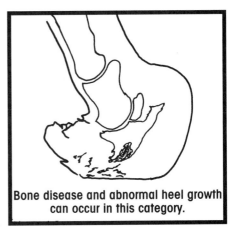

Bone disease and abnormal heel growth can occur in this category.

tendons. Their hoof capsules are often distorted with evidence of recurrent abscesses at the coronary band and heels.

How to Treat

Like the previous category, these horses should be made as comfortable as possible. Bed their stalls deeply and offer them the comfort foods described earlier. These horses are maintained on therapeutic levels of Bute, Banamine, or other potent, non-steroidal anti-inflammatory drugs.

An aggressive approach at the onset of the syndrome is required. A tenotomy is always recommended in these cases, immediately after de-rotation shoeing using the four-point aluminum rail shoe and arch support.

Prognosis

Cases at the lower end of the scale have a reasonably good prognosis for survival, provided the farrier uses good mechanics and the veterinarian performs a deep flexor tenotomy immediately.

Owners often ask me, "Is there anything that can be done to save my horse?" The answer is yes. There almost always is hope, and good treatment options are available. Explaining the options, the estimated expense, duration of treatment, and risk of losing the horse even after drastic measures are taken will help most clients reach an informed opinion. Emotional and financial commitments can be tested and surpass all expectations, and even then the horse's condition may go downhill leaving owners, veterinarians, and farriers with a feeling of loss and frustration.

On the bright side, though, to attack successfully each and every obstacle and setback through one foot or all four and have a happy camper in the end are seldom financially rewarding, but helping the horse makes up for it all.

SURGICAL OPTIONS

Horses in many of the above categories can benefit from a

surgical procedure called a deep flexor tenotomy (cutting of the tendon). This surgery is performed immediately following de-rotation shoeing and produces an optimum healing environment. The tendon severed surgically mid-cannon heals back within two to four months and the horses reach full recovery in six to 12 months.

The very sound of this procedure sends chills up the backs of those not familiar with it and what is required to make it successful. It is a big decision for owners to talk about cutting the deep flexor, as we all know what a slight bowed tendon does to an athlete. We are not thinking of an athlete at this stage, not that we can't have a sound performance animal in a year or so. It is possible and does happen, but it is a gift or bonus when that goal is achieved and it is not to be expected. Once resolved to the fact that the horse's athletic career is over, put this procedure at the top of the option list.

The success of the case rests heavily in the hands of a qualified farrier and a veterinarian with experience not only in doing such a surgical procedure, but one who has a basic knowledge of shoeing mechanics and how those mechanics relate to laminitis.

Severing the tendon and failing to address the realignment of P 3 seldom offer more than a few days of clinical improvement as the coffin bone remains trapped in a very abnormal relationship to the ground forces and P 2 above. The border of the distal apex is thin and sharp and is not designed to carry load on this surface. This procedure can be performed while the horse is standing using local anesthesia with minimum risk. Many surgeons prefer to perform the tenotomy on the table under more aseptic conditions. Either way, the end result is dependent on the farrier's ability to de-rotate properly, leaving the maximum hoof mass possible.

The toe will turn up when the horse is backed up or when in deep bedding. To avoid hyper-extension in the first 10 to 15 days after surgery, I wrap four-inch Elasticon™ down the back of the bandaged leg, across the foot, and back up the front. Three to four layers will act as additional back-up support for the tendon and it will prevent the occasional hyper-extension. Having had many cases with excessive

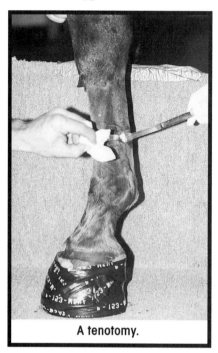

hyper-extension, I have concluded that it looks much worse than it is, as I have not seen any adverse problems from this mal-alignment.

This procedure is facilitated by the use of retractors that isolate the tendon through a one-inch incision. Using a stack of three Modified Ultimate Wedges™ over the derotation rail shoe provides enough tendon relaxation to get both retractors around the deep flexor. I keep post-operative cases in their stalls for two months and hand walk them for two months before turning them out in a small paddock. Keep them bandaged

A tenotomy.

with firm cotton wrap for at least three months to assure a better cosmetic appearance and a minimum of scar tissue. The mid-cannon site is preferred over the pastern, as it produces less luxation and preserves the lower site for future tenotomies when necessary.

Cases in the upper end of the 250-500 category who will only be used for breeding purposes are ideal candidates for this procedure as it provides 100 percent relief of the tendon pull and enhances massive sole proliferation in a very short period of time. Performed in a timely fashion with proper corrective shoeing, this procedure can prevent the progressive bone disease that typically occurs in most severe cases.

In my experience, using the tenotomy as a means of salvaging advanced stages of bone disease (grade VI to VII bone disease) is helpful, but the positive effects are short lived.

Cases cut after they have advanced bone disease seldom go more than a year before the horses develop contracted superficial tendons as well as contracted deep flexor tendons. In sum, treating laminitic horses requires not only the knowledge and skills of capable professionals but patience and dedication on the part of the owners.

In many cases, horses can recover from laminitis if they are given the opportunity to do so. Be alert, be responsive, and provide the horses with the best care possible.

CHAPTER 7

Management/Prevention

Laminitis is a very common problem. Taking a preventative approach to your horse's health might head off laminitis before it strikes. Remember that the medical emergency called laminitis results in inflammation of the laminae inside a horse's hoof. Sometimes, laminitis affects a single foot; sometimes it affects all four feet. Repeated laminitis attacks worsen the prognosis for the animal.

Several other diseases and conditions can trigger acute laminitis. Mechanical causes include:

- Road founder (too much concussion for a prolonged period of time).
- Accidents or mechanical trauma.
- Unilateral lameness, or support limb laminitis, which can develop in the weight-bearing sound limb when there is disease or trauma in the opposite limb.
- Corticosteroid therapy, which can be associated with the onset of severe laminitis.
- Using black walnut wood shavings for bedding.

Laminitis & Endotoxemia from:

- Grain founder (overeating grain).
- Grass founder (when fat horses are put in lush pastures).
- Postparturient laminitis, especially in cases where the mare has retained the placenta after giving birth.

- Water founder (when an overheated horse is allowed to tank up with water.)
- Mastitis founder (mastitis, called blue bag, affects lactating mares).
- Enteritis/colitis or endotoxic absorption (these problems crop up following surgery).
- Postoperative colic laminitis.

THE DANGERS OF OVERFEEDING

Treating laminitis is one thing, but preventing it is quite another. We do not know or understand what the mechanism is that triggers this devastating disease syndrome. However, being aware of several other clinical indications that usually proceed laminitis helps us spot the high risk patients, the ones who are predisposed to laminitis. This knowledge gives some insight into prevention.

Laminitis that is directly associated with obesity is quite easy to prevent. It's a simple formula, one I have heard so many times from old horsemen. It's a great line for maintaining a healthy horse: "The fat ones get less and the thin ones get more."

How simple this might seem. There is a great tendency for owners to overfeed their horses. They try to explain to me all the reasons why they are thoroughly convinced that their heavy animals are not only the best of the breed, but the healthiest. Apparently it is human nature for us to want to provide for our horses, much as we do for our children. Unfortunately, providing absolutely everything we think the horses might want is usually far different than what they actually need. It might give the owners a feeling of accomplishment to over-provide and over-protect, but when they go overboard they could harm their horses.

Let's use grass founder as an example. For those living in the United States east of the Mississippi River, maintaining horses on lush pastures with a balanced diet and an adequate caloric intake poses a totally different problem than maintaining a good diet for horses living in more arid areas of the Western states. It is not uncommon for lush pastures to yield up to 35% protein for several months of the year. Most people are totally unaware of the richness of their pastures. Even worse, we don't have an accurate means of knowing how much grass a horse eats in a 24-hour period.

If you want to get an idea of what they can consume, take a muck bucket or whatever is handy out to the pasture where your favorite brood mare is grazing. Pull out a large handful of grass every time she does, and put it in the basket. You'll have to work quite hard to keep up with the grazing habits of the horse, but try it for 10 to 15 minutes. In most cases, you will be amazed at the quantity of grass that one horse can, and often does, consume in a 24-hour period, especially in the spring when the days are so picture-perfect, the air so fresh, and the grass so tender and lush.

Horses can consume enormous quantities of grass.

Mother Nature has provided for us and all the little creatures of the Earth the things we need and a biological time clock to regulate our growth, maturation, ability to reproduce and replenish, age, and complete the cycle of life. We might know this, but we don't understand her management plan. How does this relate to the day-to-day maintenance of a domesticated animal, whether it's living in a stall 24 hours a day in a training stable or living the luxury life as a broodmare on hundreds of acres of manicured pastures? Today, you can walk into any library in America and find books on nutrition. Specialty magazines about horses often feature well-written articles on how to feed horses. We are a health-minded generation. We have been educated by the media to be aware of our own health. How do we become equally knowledgeable about feeding our animals? O.J.T. (on the job training) is most likely the training ground for most horse owners.

Working on horses all over the world, I am amazed at the vast range of feeding plans that are popular in different countries. In most nations, tradition runs strong and horse feeding habits haven't changed for generations. My first real eye opener was a trip to Italy. I was called in to treat a very valuable trotting stallion who was crippled from laminitis. I was amazed at his enormous size. It seemed obvious to me why he had foundered and what had to be done to him so he could walk again and, hopefully, breed more mares. Knowing how to help the stallion was one thing. Convincing its manager, veterinarian, and farrier was quite another. Of course, the language barrier added to my frustration, as I attempted to explain why the horse had developed the laminitis syndrome.

When I said, "Wow, look at this guy," they naturally assumed I was admiring the stallion for his 300-pound crest, massive body, and heavy mane that gave him a textbook image of masculinity, stamina, and strength. Little did they know that I could not believe my eyes. Before me was a Standardbred stallion who had probably weighed no more than 1,100 pounds at his racing peak. Now he topped the scale at just a pound less than a Mack truck.

Finishing the corrective shoeing and surgery, I asked the stable manager to show me what he fed the stallion. Remember, I was in Italy. They wheeled in a large cart full of lush, long stemmed grass. The cart held more than you could put in a pickup truck. They dumped the grass in the horse's paddock and I watched my patient dive into it as if he was starved. This was his mid-day feeding.

Feeding plans seem to fit our perceptions of what health is all about. In Argentina, I have watched broodmares and foals graze in lush corn fields with new corn up to their bellies. That feeding plan was far removed from the way I was taught to feed a horse, but it seemed more natural to me than graining racehorses kept in pipe corrals with not a blade of grass

Some horse people equate bulk with good health.

within 500 miles. The moral of my story is that man and beast are amazingly adaptable creatures, genetically ingrained to survive.

I feel there is a worldwide tendency for people to over-provide food for their horses. Take a moment to think about the horses that live in the most desolate, rugged, arid areas of America. They do not depend on man in any fashion to survive. Our feral horses are called Mustangs, but few strains of pure wild horses exist today. Most of these Western horses are simply the wild offspring of domestic horses. Their ancestors were set free for various reasons over the past 400 years. If you study Mustang herds closely, you can see a resemblance to most major breeds.

A veterinarian friend of mine, Dr. Thomas Hartgrove, had the opportunity to examine closely the intestinal contents of a hundred Mustangs that had been living in the desert near Las Vegas, Nevada. Amazingly, no sand and no parasites were found in the intestinal tracts of these wild animals. Domesticated horses living in that area are frequently found with sand and parasites. Sand colic is a great concern for the horsemen and veterinarians in areas with a lot of sand. What can this possibly tell us? I am certain there is more that we need to learn about a sound nutritional plan.

I think we have lost sight of what a healthy horse looks

like. By taking a look at the market for young horses, it quickly becomes evident that current standards for body weight are less than ideal. Many people in the horse industry are beginning to agree with me. We are pushing young horses too hard and too fast. Every year, I see an alarming number of show Quarter horses only old enough to show in halter classes, who have already developed life-threatening laminitis. Most simply do not survive, despite the heroic recovery efforts, simply because of their tremendous muscle and enormous bulk. The same mechanics that easily might reverse the crippling effects of laminitis for horses that weigh a 1,000 pounds will not touch horses of the same build that weigh in at 1,500 to 1,800 pounds.

When I look closely at the feed programs that owners think will make their horses competitive in halter classes, it seems amazing to me that only a small percentage of the horses tip the scale and fall prey to laminitis. Unfortunately, many will be at the top of their class. Broodmares and stallions that routinely carry more

Putting a fat horse in a dry lot can save its life.

than 200 pounds excess weight should be considered high risk. However, it is generally thought that laminitis only strikes someone else's horse and seldom hits home. It's called "bad luck" when it does. I firmly believe that we make our own luck. Ignore caution lights for high risk horses and you can lose one or more of your best horses to laminitis.

I have watched successful breeding operations fold due to the loss of their "ace in the hole," the one mare or stallion that paid the bills to keep the stable going. At first, that horse might have only had "...a touch of laminitis," but if it had poor quality feet and was grossly overweight, then in six weeks it was dead. This story is repeated over and over with the same catastrophic ending.

What do you need to do to get a handle on your horses' feed program? Start by taking an unbiased view of your entire operation, then assess each horse individually. Work with nutrition specialists who are highly focused and dedicated to making a better tomorrow for you and your horses. Why not lean on someone who lives and breathes nutrition? Body tapes are reasonably accurate and are very helpful for monitoring weight. You could buy a set of scales and weigh your animals on a regular basis. Or you could use the truck scales at your local feed dealer when convenient. You soon will learn what a hundred pounds of added weight looks like on a 1,000-pound horse or a 600-pound weanling.

Does your exercise program complement your feed program and vise versa? Do you feed the same amount of grain to each of your horses, regardless of what they really need? Can you put your fattest horses out on a dry lot with the feeling that you are doing the best thing for them? Most people cannot. I try to refrain from using the descriptive word "fat" when looking at a client's horses. I might get in less trouble if I called someone's husband or wife fat rather than using that word to describe their favorite horse. Terms like "exceptionally stout," "handsomely bulked up," and "gorgeous power house," keep my clients happy, but diplomatically gets my point across.

MINIMIZING THE RISK OF OPPOSING LIMB LAMINITIS

Laminitis caused by opposing limb breakdown also can be prevented in many instances with proper management. What are the kinds of injuries that can trigger opposing limb founder, which is more correctly called unilateral laminitis?

• Any injury that will require more than two weeks to heal puts a horse at risk.

• Deep puncture wounds to the navicular area.

• Extensive fractures of P 1, P 2, and P 3.

• Fetlock breakdowns, shattered sesamoids.

• Unilateral paralysis

• Complicated septic lower joints and/or tendon sheath. Any horse that is persistently lame for three to five days quickly becomes a high risk candidate for laminitis. Septic joints, particularly hocks and stifles, seem to predispose the foot on the opposing limb to laminitis. It sometimes occurs in the previously "sound" leg within days of the first signs of pain or lameness in the "bad" leg. In such cases of traumatic laminitis, the laminae become dysfunctional due to lack of blood flow.

How does standing for hours, days, or weeks on one foot, while protecting the injured leg, affect blood flow to that foot? Performing venograms on normal feet, I have found a marked absence of contrast throughout the lamellar vessels when the foot is bearing weight at the time the dye is injected. Apparently, the weight of the horse is precariously balanced between

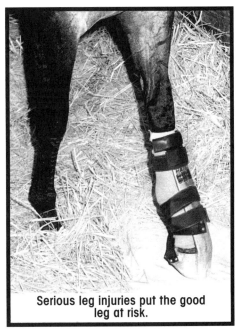

Serious leg injuries put the good leg at risk.

the deep flexor tendon and laminae. Once loaded, the laminae stretch to their normal physiological limit, which apparently mechanically restricts normal blood flow. When an injured horse stands planted on its good foot for endless hours or days, its body weight shuts down the adequate nutrients to the laminae in the "good" foot, which soon become dysfunctional.

Observing unilateral cases, I have determined that horses that constantly shift back and forth from one leg to the other are much less likely to have laminitis than those that cock the "bad" leg and stand like that all day. Proper management of such cases can prevent opposing limb laminitis in the majority of cases. Reducing tendon pull at the very onset of injury can help prevent ischemia, or the cell death from the blocked blood supply, that causes lamellar death. Use of the Modified Ultimate Wedge provides the mechanics that can help prevent unilateral lameness. It is crucial to take into consideration the toe angle, heel angle, ventral angle, cup of foot, and overall quality and health of horn before beginning this corrective shoeing. Failure to do so can cause several problems.

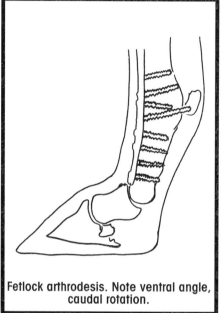

Fetlock arthrodesis. Note ventral angle, caudal rotation.

I believe waiting until radiographic signs of laminitis are present before applying a mechanical aid seldom offers favorable results. Then the special shoeing mechanics is too little, too late. Normally, the first six to eight weeks following an acute injury is the high-risk period, even if the original injury is responding quite favorably. Many times the foot balance on the injured leg goes off scale as well, putting these cases in double jeopardy.

After a shattered fetlock has been repaired surgically, the horse will have a tendency to develop a very low heel and tipped up coffin bone on the injured limb (caudal rotation), which often predisposes the horse to further problems as P 1, P 2 and P 3 luxates. The severe luxation, or mis-alignment of these bones, can create abnormal stress on the supporting tendon. Unfortunately, this simply adds insult to injury, especially if the good foot has developed traumatic laminitis. On the bright side, though, caudal rotation in the leg in which surgery was performed can be prevented with proper therapeutic shoeing when addressed at the onset.

Most traumatic unilateral cases are classic sinkers. Seldom do they have more than a few degrees of rotation. They often are seen to have 2 centimeters of sinking.

Once laminitis is evident, treat it accordingly. Reverse the forces at play. Unfortunately, most horses that develop unilateral laminitis have severe damage when they are diagnosed. Most score 800 or better on the given scale. Swift, aggressive mechanics can pull many through, but it is a very costly and high-risk treatment.

Frequent radiographs and constant monitoring of the good foot is quite important for a successful preventative program.

CHAPTER 8

Case Studies

The following are case studies which illustrate the kinds of challenges posed by laminitis and how I addressed each of them. Some of them required just simple mechanics; others tested my ingenuity. All provided an invaluable learning experience.

CASE NO. 1 (PONY)

Years ago, renowned horse trainer Vincent O'Brien brought me to Ireland to look at foot problems affecting some of his racehorses. While I was there, the very young son of trainer Tommy Stack ran up to me with great excitement. The boy had a most sincere request, and I will never forget the look on his face when he asked me, "Mister, will you look at my pony?"

I said, "Yes. What kind of problem does it have?" He replied, "He has wind balls (windpuffs) and terrible laminitis." I said, "Well go get him."

He took off at a dead run, as excited as a kid could be. Twenty minutes later, I saw him coming up the shed row, dragging a poor little foundered pony that could hardly walk. His pony had grass foundered due to being put out on a rich pasture and being overweight, which is very common with ponies.

The pony's feet had grown long and misshapen in a very typical fashion for laminitis cases. Its toes were curled up and its heels were crushed underneath. The pony walked with its front feet well out in front, in a very slow, reluctant fashion. The pony obviously was in pain.

By that time, having treated literally hundreds of chronic laminitis cases, I realized how easy it would be to help this pony mechanically. Radiographs were not taken for the sake of time, but having a thorough knowledge of the anatomy and how laminitis alters or distorts the hoof capsule and damages other sensitive areas, I had insight into what had to be done mechanically to reverse the destructive forces at work.

The first thing I did was remove the heels starting at the point of the frog and back. Then I reduced the breakover by several inches by trimming the toe away from the ground surface, which created a rocker toe and immediately relieved the tremendous pull of the deep flexor tendon on the coffin bone. Then I applied a wedge to the newly trimmed foot to further reduce tendon pull and the pony became quite comfortable immediately.

Being able to help this youngster's pony was as fulfilling and gratifying to me as helping the most famous racehorse that I have ever worked on.

CASE NO. 2 (THOROUGHBRED BROODMARE)

I once received a call from England concerning a mare with laminitis who appeared to be in desperate shape and was facing euthanasia. The mare was a very special little Thoroughbred named Mrs. Moss. She had been purchased by Lady Tavistock for a mere £1,200 Sterling. Being bred to several nice stallions over the next few years, Mrs. Moss produced four stakes winners, three of which were group winners. Her record won the hearts of horsemen all over Europe. She had been voted Broodmare of the Year on more than one occasion.

Sadly, all of her fame and prestige did not make her immune

to the ill effects of unilateral laminitis. When my wife and I arrived at Woburn Abbey, Lady Tavistock's home, we were immediately taken to see the mare. I found a small group around her that included her farrier, veterinarian, handler, stud groom, and other concerned caretakers. Their faces told a sad story, but they were more than eager to learn what I would have to say, especially if I could offer an option other than euthanasia.

I will never forget the satisfaction I felt the moment I touched the foot and picked it up for a closer look. The mare had unilateral laminitis in a chronic club foot. Her sole was bulging well below the hoof wall because the coffin bone had penetrated the sole. A chronic draining track indicated she had long-term osteomyelitis as well. She also had several abscesses at the coronary band due to osteomyelitis.

I thought, "What a piece of cake, Redden." I wondered how I was going to tell everyone how easy it would be to fix the problem. I explained that this one was a keeper and simple mechanical alterations would give her a new lease on life and that she should live a reasonably normal life with a little special care and concern from all taking care of her. I shod the mare in less than 30 minutes with a four point variety shoe that relieved the stress on her foot. I realigned the coffin bone, then raised the heel and changed the breakover forces to reduce tendon pull.

I assured everyone that the exposed coffin bone was just a temporary clinical finding and was not permanent nor had to be terminal. Everyone was elated with the news, but remained a bit skeptical, even though the little mare appeared to walk with less pain with the shoe I had put on. Realizing I could easily fly back to Kentucky the same night, I asked for a ride to Heathrow airport. Lady Tavistock insisted that we spend the evening, as she wanted to know more about what I did and why.

When news about the mare's "miraculous" recovery became known, it opened doors for me in Europe, New

Zealand, and many other countries. I will be forever grateful that I cared for Mrs. Moss. I've gone back to England many times over the years and have always taken the time to look in on her. I was so pleased to see her live out her last days with three good feet and one that did almost as well with the corrective shoeing, despite the fact that it had almost prematurely ended her life.

It has not always been easy for me to feel the magic of basic physics as it relates to the equine foot, but it gets easier as it has been one of life's learning experiences. Helping others, I sincerely feel that laminitis, a seemingly impossible problem of yesterday, can be a "piece of cake" to treat successfully. Putting good horses back on their feet in the cases I work on today are just as gratifying to me as it was to help Mrs. Moss comfortably live out her final years.

CASE NO. 3 (NIJINSKY II)

One morning, I got a call around 6 a.m. from a good friend and insurance adjuster. He told me that Nijinsky II had foundered and needed help. Nijinsky was one of the world's leading Thoroughbred sires. Breeding a top mare to this outstanding racehorse and tremendously successful stallion was the dream of most horsemen.

At the time, I did not have a scale to classify the laminitis syndrome, but it was quite clear to me, as it was to the several other veterinarians called in, that the problem was serious and posed a very real threat to the horse's life. Nijinsky was suffering from excessive rotation of the coffin bone in both front feet. He had other severe clinical signs and was in extreme pain.

Working closely with the late Dr. Walter Kaufman and with Clay Arnold, Nijinsky's long time caretaker, we were successful in treating the course of the syndrome despite coffin bones that were all but penetrating both feet. I shod Nijinsky with sole support pads designed to enhance breakover. I performed a partial wall re-sectioning to alleviate sub-solar ab-

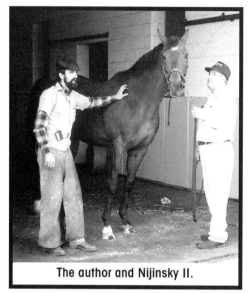

The author and Nijinsky II.

scesses. This stallion had good, strong feet, which aided the prognosis. However, he also suffered from lymphangitis of one hind limb, which complicated the situation. Treating the lymphangitis required regular exercise, but treating the laminitis required stall rest.

Nijinsky responded to my treatment. The horse was able to stand at stud for an additional six years, and enjoyed a good quality life until he was euthanized due to the infirmities of old age.

CASE NO. 4 (THOROUGHBRED MARE)

Central Kentucky Thoroughbred breeder Dr. Smiser West once sent his son Bob looking for me when one of his best mares was in the throws of a life-threatening episode of traumatic laminitis. Several weeks before, another horse had run over her in a race and lacerated a rear tendon quite badly. The tendon sheath became infected with pseudomonas and suddenly became a life-threatening problem in itself. The tendon began to show a favorable response after several weeks of intense therapy. About the time it appeared to be out of the woods — bang — the mare was totally non-weight bearing on the opposite hind foot.

It was a cold, bitter winter day and Doc West was desperate for a second opinion as everyone else had recommended euthanasia. At that time, I had never met Doc, as he was called. He was a retired dentist, a self-made man with a ton of experience and good country logic. Together we examined the foot on this very nice mare and I felt we had a good shot at turning it around, even though the hoof capsule was all but off.

I spent approximately three hours in sub-zero weather fabricating an emergency device that would hold us until morning. Once my mind got going in overdrive, the cold was never a problem for us, just tough on my help.

Arriving the next morning, I found my patient suffering from serious diarrhea and giving off the typical smell of salmonella. That day, I worked on the foot under an umbrella, as she would periodically lift her tail and squirt 20 feet. Doc left for Nassau and said, "Call me if you have to put her down."

My good friend, the veterinarian Richard Holder, managed to get the diarrhea under control. I was elated that we had crossed a major hurdle and I thought the rest would be a piece of cake. Visibly Different was her name and was she ever. I had her on my mind day and night, scanning every potential option that had more possibilities.

I ended up removing a majority of the hoof because of gangrene. I fashioned a temporary prosthesis that was attached the moment I had a few cornified spots of the hoof to hold it. The entire sole was gone and white bone was exposed in places, but the coronary band appeared to be quite healthy.

Applying the first prosthesis was a real challenge, as we had to wait for her to lie down. I sedated her and went to work

Working on Visibly Different some months later.

with Hank Murphy and Cookie holding the leg. Designing and fabricating at a job site is always tough, as you are constantly compromising your technique due to the lack of proper tools and supplies. All went well, though, until the acrylic that I used to anchor the device started curing. Visibly Different felt the heat and began to kick violently with a capital V. Hank held on as long as he could and we all dove for cover. This work can be life threatening to the vet, farrier, and caretaker, as well as the horse (be careful, think safety). Before she got up, she managed to kick the wall real hard a couple of times, demolishing my three hours of work and the prosthesis and leaving half of her coffin bone stuck on the wall in a bloody mess.

I will never forget Doc saying, "Dr. Redden, what do we do now?" I replied, "Put on the coffee. We're going to need a few pots to get through the night," and we started all over again.

Visibly Different was my first, exceptionally challenging case and we all felt the thrill of victory six months later when she had a new hoof. Her first foal sold for $340,000, and she has had 12 since. I looked after her for years and was finally able to turn her over to the farm farrier. I have not seen the mare for some time, but she still stays on my mind and gives me a little nudge if I get a sinking feeling on a tough case.

I cannot thank Dr. West enough for giving me all the confidence in the world. I am certain he did not think we would make it, but he sincerely felt that if effort was all it took, we just might succeed. I have had other cases for Doc West since then that we haven't been as lucky with. But my philosophy is, if you are going to hit the wall, hit it high and don't get caught at the bottom for not trying.

CASE NO. 5 (RACE FILLY)

I recently examined a very valuable race filly who was suffering from acute laminitis. I saw her only a few hours from onset. Examining her with the attending veterinarian, we found she had 10 degrees of rotation, horn-lamellar space of

20 to 25 mm on one foot and 25 to 30 mm on the other, 4 mm soles, and a faint coronary band halo. She was quite lame and did not want her foot picked up.

Whoa, how much can a big dog weigh? I never saw so much damage in a pair of feet on a horse that worked in blazing time a few days previously. Her blood work showed that she had been super stressed and was suffering from some kind of metabolic disorder. She was grade III-plus lame, would walk if you stayed after her, and the imprint of P 3 could be clearly seen on the soles of both feet. The coronary bands felt within normal limits, but were very sensitive. I did not put testers on the feet (note: you do not use testers to confirm laminitis, they only make the patient hate you. Use other parameters that are more meaningful anyway. Be kind and compassionate when examining and treating very painful animals.)

Taking radiographs and applying wedges and arch support was a bit chaotic, as the filly was so uncomfortable. I applied the emergency aid on the worst foot first. Within minutes I could pick up the opposite foot with ease. Chalk up a positive — within minutes, the filly was standing much more relaxed and had a bright, alert eye.

Radiographs showed that she was compressed to the max and most likely producing serum and creating even more damage to the sole corium, laminae, and bone. She had a history of laminitis, but appeared to have a full recovery and raced several times, winning in top-class company. We suspected that she had to have pre-existing lesions. Although this degree of displacement can occur in hours, it is rare and goes with a totally different set of clinical circumstances.

The big question was, when did it occur —days or weeks ago? I performed a venogram, which is a diagnostic procedure I developed with the help of Dr. Chris Pollitt that assesses circulation in the foot. It was quite apparent that the lamellar scar was very old, as the scar tissue was well established. The lamellar vessels, coronary plexus, circumflex vessels, and terminal arch all appeared within normal limits. The farrier who had shod her a few times related that she had a dropped sole that was very flat, with a slight bulge and a real wide sole-horn junction (yellow line). Backing the toes up to examine further and opening the sole-wall junction, I found bright red blood — no serum and no pus. This further confirmed that the majority, if not all, of the radiographic lesions were pre-existing for weeks, possibly months.

Yes, she had acute laminitis, with a shaky history. It was a puzzling case, though. Top racehorses just do not race well with excessive displacement of P 3, but this one obviously did.

Remember, all is possible, even though rare. Don't discount anything. Know your starting point, talk with the farrier. He or she knows the particulars like the back of his hand. Put all the clues together. The venogram acted as a major diagnostic tool for this case. Without it, time would have given us the answers we needed. But

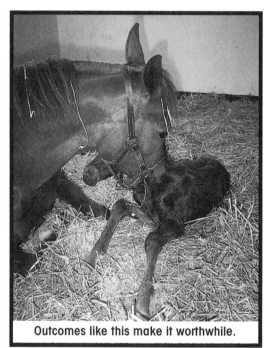

Outcomes like this make it worthwhile.

many times the wait and see attitude assures total disaster. Study the details and don't be afraid to say, "I was wrong." We have all made quick decisions based on our own experience and knowledge of the subject and judgment, but it is the prerogative of a good veterinarian or farrier to change the course of thinking as circumstances demand.

Helping others with laminitic horses has been very rewarding, but also very humbling, as some of my very best efforts over the years have not reached my personal goals for the horses, nor the clients, as I have hit the wall hard many times and it hurts for a long time.

While I lick my wounds, I take each unsuccessful case apart piece by piece and examine the sheer mechanics inside and out. Invariably, each failure teaches me something that will help the next laminitic horse I treat. I hear some of my colleagues in various places of the world, consider me controversial, as I am always changing my mind. I consider that a compliment. I feel we have only touched the surface of understanding the laminitis syndrome. I am never satisfied with status quo, even when it does exceed the limits of traditional standards.

Knowledge comes from experience and better judgment from making mistakes. I encourage young farriers and veterinarians not to be afraid of failures. They can spur you on to successes as you treat the horse, the noblest of species.

Radiographic Techniques

Here's a note for veterinarians on how to take series of radiographs of a laminitic horse. We know what we need to see — pure lateral views with soft tissue detail. Initially, we want a baseline series that shows the starting point, then radiographs taken periodically during the treatment phase. The veterinarian, and farrier need to see a good, clear lateral view of the entire foot in order to establish the position of P 1, P 2 and P 3.

How do we consistently get good radiographs?

First, measure the distance from the center of the primary beam to the ground on your portable machine (cross hair). The wooden block used for the lateral view must be within one inch of the height of the center beam. Using two blocks, one for each foot, certainly helps most lame horses stand more comfortably.

Since you are trying to measure the angle of rotation, you'll want to put a reference mark on the hoof. A wire embedded in the long dimension of the block makes a consistent ground level opaque marker when shooting bare feet. The shoe is the marker for a shod horse. Before you take the radiographs, sedate the horse with a light does of Dormosedan™ (.25cc per 1,000 pounds of body weight is a good light dose). Contrast paste makes a good opaque marker down the center line of the hoof wall. So does wire.

Place the horse's feet on the blocks. The blocks must be in a flat plane with the machine. Level ground is desirable, but not totally necessary. Your goal should be for the primary beam to strike the hoof capsule within a half-inch of the ventral surface of P 3. I refer to the clinch line as a target. This will reveal one branch of the shoe and perfectly superimposed wings of P 3, provided that the medial-lateral balance is good. These image parameters must be met in order to measure accurately sole depth, rotation, sinking, and posterior displacement of P 3.

A good teaching exercise is to sedate a horse, put the foot on a number of blocks with different heights, keeping all other variables the same, and measure the same soft tissue zone mentioned above in precisely the same plane.

To prevent unwarranted magnification, you must have zero film-subject distance to minimize image distortion. Make sure you maintain a 90-degree beam-to-film projection and remember, there is only a small area of the film centered around the primary beam that represents true image. The rest will have slight to moderate distortion.

Positioning, film-screen detail, and developing are three basic areas that require a disciplined, methodical approach to assure consistent, repeatable, high-quality radiographs. Yes, it requires precision and good practice. High-quality radiographs are great tools for the veterinarian and farrier to use. The radiographs will help the horse's owner and care givers better understand what is happening to the horse.

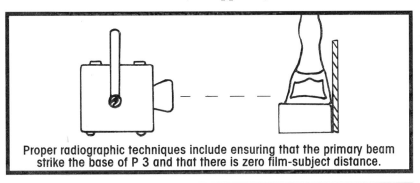

Proper radiographic techniques include ensuring that the primary beam strike the base of P 3 and that there is zero film-subject distance.

FREQUENTLY ASKED QUESTIONS

What caused my horse to founder?

There are typical cases that follow typical history. Unfortunately, a large majority of cases have an unknown etiology. In my experience, laminitis is always secondary to another disease process. It can be triggered by colic, Potomac horse fever, salmonella, stress, retained placenta, or a traumatic injury. Laminitis also can be triggered by obesity and over eating.

How do I know if my horse has laminitis?

It might be more difficult to answer this question than you think as there are numerous variables that affect the horse with a bilateral laminitic stance. Confirming the fact that your horse has laminitis appears to be straight forward, but is often confused with other similar bilateral lamenesses. Being absolutely, 100% positive that your horse has laminitis is not as important the first few hours or days as treating him long before you are certain of the diagnosis. The typical laminitic stance — with the horse standing with the feet out front and the hind feet underneath and reluctant to move — sounds the alarm. You have an emergency. Radiographs can aid in the diagnosis and treatment.

How can I prevent my horse from getting laminitis?

Having a poor understanding of what really triggers laminitis leaves us handicapped in our ability to prevent the disease syndrome. There are known circumstances that can trigger laminitis that we can control and, in a sense, help us reduce the risk. These include obesity, which normally is a management problem which must be addressed and corrected with each and every individual. Maximum mechanical protection of the sound leg when there is a severe injury in the other leg also can help prevent or minimize the onset of laminitis.

Once a horse founders, is he likely to founder again?

No, not unless the horse encounters similar conditions or circumstances that led to the first episode. However, many horse people worldwide believe that laminitis is a recurring problem. That's because many times the horse develops complications months from onset that may appear to be a new bout of laminitis, when actually it is a continuation or progression of the original onset. Those horses that do have true, recurrent laminitis have a poor prognosis the second time, particularly if they were left with permanent scarring damage to the laminae.

When can my horse be ridden or exercised?

The mind set must be modified at this stage. You must forget about exercise of any kind, until your horse has stopped deteriorating and progressed well into the recovery stage. This can be as quick as 45 days with minimum insult and up to 1½ years for full recovery.

Why do many professionals view laminitis as a hopeless situation?

I hear this one every day and the answer is quite simple: treating complicated laminitis is not everyone's cup of tea. No one gains adequate knowledge of the subject without the benefit of good experience. Seeing a multitude of cases and having consistent bad luck is worse than no experience at all. It becomes very discouraging and tunnel vision sets in. Euthanasia is not part of my treatment regime but, unfortunately, is the first choice for many other people in a complicated case of laminitis.

When do I throw in the towel?

When the decision to stop treating the horse has been made. When all viable options have been exercised and the horse continues to painfully go downhill. Be careful here though. I hear "We did everything and nothing worked" all the time. Reinventing the wheel has dangerous consequences. Use known basic principles and be alert to all small, positive, as well as negative responses to therapy.

Will my farrier be able to shoe my laminitic horse the right way?

Your farrier could best answer that. This is not a show-and-tell technique, regardless of the expertise and ability of your farrier. There is a learning curve for all pathological shoeing, just as there is for all routine good shoeing techniques. Good experience and education in the field of pathological shoeing is necessary for the cross over. This goes for you, your veterinarian, as well as your farrier. Most likely, both are concerned with a multitude of routine problems that are not associated with pathological shoeing in any fashion.

"Do you have good experience with complicated laminitis cases? How many do you normally see in a week, a month, a year? What is the degree of insult to these cases and what are they like one year later?"

QUESTIONS HORSE OWNERS SHOULD ASK THEIR VETERINARIAN

"Do you have good experience with complicated laminitis cases?

How many do you normally see in a week, a month, a year?

What is the degree of insult to these cases and what are they like one year later?"

This will put everyone on the same wave length. Any one of the trio — owner, veterinarian, and farrier — armed with good, sound knowledge can carry the other two, provided there is intense desire to win. Of course, it is best for everyone to have good experience and dozens of successful cases behind them. That is not likely for owners. We simply do not have an organized curriculum for equine podiatry. Hopefully the 21st Century will change all that.

GLOSSARY

Basal cells — One of the cells of the deep layer of the epithelium, found within the basement membrane.

Breakover — Phase of the stride in which the heel is lifted and the foot "rolls over" the toe.

Carbohydrate overload — Excessive high-energy dietary component that consists of simple and complex sugars. Grains are high-carbohydrate feeds.

Circumflex artery — Lies under the base of P 3 and along the parameter of the bone.

Coffin bone (pedal bone, P 3) — Bone within the hoof.

Coronary band — Rim of specialized skin around the top of the hoof wall. Includes the coronary corium and blood vessels.

Corticosteroids — Potent anti-inflammatory drugs, which also can suppress the immune response.

Deep flexor tendon — Tendon that attaches to a muscle at the back of the forearm or thigh, runs down the back of the leg, and attaches onto the bottom of the pedal bone.

Dermal laminae — Layers or folds of tissue; e.g., the tiny corrugations that are attached to the coffin bone by a tough, fibrous bond. They carry the blood and nutrients to the hoof capsule, and interlock with the epidermal laminae attached to the hoof wall.

Derotation — Realigning P 3 with the normal load plane (normal ventral angle) and the proximal digits.

Digital artery — Arteries that carry blood to the feet, found along the medial and lateral sides of the pastern.

Epidermal laminae — Layers or folds of horn tissue; e.g. the corrugations found along the inside of the hoof capsule. They interlock with the dermal laminae.

Epithelial cells — Cells which cover the surface of the body and line its cavities.

Foramina — Plural of foramen. A natural hole or passage, especially one into or through a bone. A natural port for blood vessels to pass.

Founder — Commonly overused lay term for laminitis. From the nautical use, meaning to fill with water and sink.

Hoof capsule — The horny shell found below the coronary band, consisting of wall, sole, frog, bars, and bulbs of heel.

Horn-lamellar zone — The space found between the outer face of the wall and the face of P 3. This zone is a critical area to monitor with laminitis.

Impar ligament — Dense, fibrous structure that connects the navicular bone to the coffin bone.

Ischemia — Localized cell death caused by blocked blood supply.

Laminitis — Painful foot condition in which the blood supply of the hoof wall is interrupted, and the hoof wall-coffin bone bond breaks down. Also called founder.

Navicular bone — Small bone at the back of the coffin joint.

Navicular bursa — Small, fluid-filled sac between the back of the navicular bone and the deep digital flexor tendon.

Obesity, as cause — An increase in body weight beyond the limitations of skeletal and physical requirements, as the result of an excessive accumulation of fat in the body.

Ossification — The formation of bone or of a bony substance. The conversion of fibrous tissue or of cartilage into bone or a bony substance.

Osteomyelitis — Bone infection and destruction, usually caused by bacterial invasion of a damaged bone.

Penetration, of coffin bone — The sole ruptures due to the descending coffin bone, exposing sole corium.

Periople — Thin, cuticle-like layer that covers the top part of the hoof wall, just below the coronary band.

Phenylbutazone (Bute) — Medication with potent, anti-inflammatory, antipyretic, and analgesic properties.

Rotation — The process of turning around an axis; e.g., the coffin bone rotates around the distal end of P 2, or the coffin bone rotates downward away from the parallel relationship of the hoof wall.

Supporting limb laminitis — Laminitis that develops in the "good" foot when a horse tries to unload the injured or diseased foot or limb.

Suspensory ligament — Ligament that originates at the back of the knee/hock and cannon bone, runs down the back of the cannon bone, and divides into two branches that attach onto the top and outside of the sesamoid bones.

Sesamoid bones — A small, flat bone developed in a tendon, which moves over a bony surface. Two found at the back of the fetlock.

Sinker — Massive lamellar death in which the bond between the hoof wall and the coffin bone becomes dysfunctional and P 3 sinks.

Sole corium — Tissue that produces the horn, which forms the insensitive layer of the sole.

Stratum internum — The innermost, non-pigmented zone of the wall.

Stratum medium — The zone of horn wall found between the stratum tectorium and stratum intermission. Pigmented zone with slightly less dense tubule formation.

Stratum tectorium — Dense outer layer of the hoof wall.

Suppurative — Producing pus.

Tenotomy — A surgical procedure in which a tendon is cut.

Terminal arch — Of, pertain to, or forming a boundary, limit, or end. Curved.

Tubule — A minute tube.

Venogram — A procedure developed with Dr. Chris Pollitt which aids in assessing blood supply in the foot.

INDEX

ACKNOWLEDGEMENTS

I would like to thank my wife, Nancy, and my longtime friend and colleague, Dr. Dick Mansmann, for their persistent insistence that I write a book teaching my concepts and techniques.

The Blood-Horse has been extremely helpful over the years and I thank the magazine and its staff for their support. Kim Herbert, editor of *The Horse*, paved the way to make this book possible and without the sincere dedication and expertise of Jackie Duke, it would not have been possible, as she has diligently helped me pull my thoughts together and put them in book form.

I cannot thank Marsha Glass, my private secretary, enough for her ability to quickly transfer my late night scribbling into disk format, meeting all deadlines with a smile.

My patients and their owners have made it all possible and I do thank everyone of them, along with those I have failed to mention.

RECOMMENDED READINGS

Brega, J. The Horse: the Foot. Shoeing & Lameness. London: J.A. Allen, 1995.

King, C. Equine Lameness. Grand Prairie, Tex.: Equine Research, 1997.

Leach, D, Moyer, W, and Pollitt, CC. Equine Lameness and Foot Conditions, Refresher Course for Veterinarians. Post Graduate Committee in Veterinary Science, University of Sydney, 1990.

Mansmann, RA and Miller, PS. Instructions for Equine Clients. St. Louis: Mosby-Year Book, Inc., 1995.

Pollitt, CC. Color Atlas of the Horse's Hoof. London: Mosby-Wolfe, 1995.

Rooney, JR, Rev. The Lame Horse, updated & expanded ed. Neenah, Wisc.: Russell Meerdink Co., 1997.

Stashak, TS. Adams' Lameness in Horses, 4th ed. Philadelphia: Lea & Febiger, 1987.

Stashak, TS. Horseowner's Guide to Lameness. Baltimore, Md.: Williams & Wilkins, 1996.

Yovich, JV. Ed. The Veterinary Clinics of North America: Equine Practice: The Equine Foot. Philadelphia, April 1989.

Redden, RF. Refurbishing the Poor Quality Hoof. Proceedings Bluegrass Laminitis Symposium. Louisville, Ky. 1996.

Redden, RF. Four-Point Techniques, Concepts and Concerns; Laminitis and Derotation Revisited; Laminitis Protocol. Proceedings Bluegrass Laminitis Symposium. Louisville, Ky. 1997.

Redden, RF. Superficial Flexor Tenotomy as a Means for Treating Complicated Laminitis and Flexor Deformity; Going the Last Mile with Difficult Cases.. Proceedings Bluegrass Laminitis Symposium. Louisville, Ky. 1998.

Redden, RF. Shoeing the Laminitic Horse. Proceedings American Association of Equine Practitioners. Phoenix, Ariz. 1997.

Redden, RF. The Four-Point Trim.

Redden, RF. Shoeing the Laminitic Horse

Laminitis sites on the Internet

The Horse Interactive: http://www.thehorse.com

Hoofcare & Lameness: http://www.hoofcare.com

The Holistic Horse: http://www. holistichorse.com

The Haynet: http://www.haynet.net

American Farrier's Association: http://www.amfarriers.com

American Association of Equine Practitioners
    Client Education articles:
    http://www.aaep.org/client.htm

The Equine Connection: The National AAEP Locator
    Service:
    http://www.getadvm.com/equcon.html

Sport Horse Biomechanics and Effects of Shoeing studies
    at Michigan State University:
    http://www.cvm.msu.edu/dressage

The Hoof Project at Texas A&M:
    http://www.cvm.tamu.edu/hoof

Picture Credits

CHAPTER 2
Anne M. Eberhardt, 14, 16, 18, 25; Ric Redden DVM, 18, 24, 25; *The Horse*, 22.

CHAPTER 3
Tina McGregor, DVM, 29; Ric Redden, 31, 42, 43.

CHAPTER 4
Ric Redden, 48, 49, 52, 54; Anne M. Eberhardt, 51; Barbara D. Livingston, 51.

CHAPTER 5
Ric Redden, 62, 63, 65-72, 75, 78.

CHAPTER 6
Anne M. Eberhardt, 82, 83, 87; Ric Redden, 92, 97.

CHAPTER 7
Anne M. Eberhardt, 108, 111; Ric Redden, 110; Equi-Photo, 113.

CHAPTER 8
Ric Redden, 120, 121.

EDITOR — JACQUELINE DUKE
COVER/BOOK DESIGN — SUZANNE C. DEPP
ASSISTANT ILLUSTRATOR — JEFF BURKHART
COVER PHOTO—ANNE M. EBERHARDT

About the Author

Ric Redden is considered one of the foremost authorities and pioneers on the subject of laminitis. A lifelong horseman, Redden is among the few equine practitioners who also is a trained farrier. As such, he has successfully welded his practical understanding of the horse's foot with a scientist's training.

A Kentucky native, Redden spent much of his youth living on

a farm. He went to work at an early age after his father, a minister, suffered a serious back injury. Redden graduated from high school in his junior year and attended pre-veterinary school at Eastern Kentucky University. During this time, he shod and galloped horses in Central Kentucky. While serving in the U.S. Army, he rode and shod the horses of the U.S. pentathlon team in San Antonio, Texas.

Ric Redden, DVM

Redden graduated in 1974 from The Ohio State University School of Veterinary Medicine with an award of excellence in equine surgery and medicine. After school, he started a racetrack practice focused on lameness. His success as a lameness diagnostician made him a sought-after consultant and he traveled to many racing centers to treat patients.

In 1983, Redden fulfilled a longtime dream when he opened his International Equine Podiatry Center, the only clinic in the world devoted exclusively to foot work. He wears a shoeing apron and works the fire, building therapeutic shoes, braces, and even prosthetic limbs. Redden recently was inducted into the International Equine Veterinarians Hall of Fame.

He has treated hundreds of horses over the years, including such famous Thoroughbreds as Nijinsky II and Habitat. He also has developed many foot products used by veterinarians and farriers worldwide. Redden annually hosts the Laminitis Symposium, which draws an international group of partici-pants. He is much in demand as a speaker and clinician.

He and his wife Nancy and their children live outside Versailles, Kentucky.

The Horse Health Library

**Other Titles in
The Horse Health Care Library:**
($14.95 each)

■ Understanding EPM

■ Understanding Equine First Aid

■ Understanding the Equine Foot

■ Understanding Equine Lameness

■ Understanding Equine Nutrition

**Coming in
The Horse Health Care Library:**
($14.95 each)

■ Understanding Basic Horse Care

■ Understanding the Broodmare

■ Understanding the Stallion

■ Understanding the Foal

■ Understanding the Older Horse

■ Understanding Equine Behavior

**Videos from
The Blood-Horse
New Video Collection:**
($39.95 each)

■ Conformation:
   How to Buy a Winner

■ First Aid for Horses

■ Lameness in the Horse

■ Owning Thoroughbreds

■ Sales Preparation

To order call 800-582-5604
(In Kentucky call 606-278-2361)